THE LITURGY FOR TEENS

MEENA AWAD

THE LITURGY FOR TEENS

by

Meena Awad

ST SHENOUDA'S PRESS
SYDNEY, AUSTRALIA
2020

THE LITURGY FOR TEENS

ST SHENOUDA PRESS
8419 Putty Rd,
Putty, NSW, 2330

www.stshenoudapress.com

ISBN 13: 978-0-6485754-2-9

About the Author:

Meena Awad is a member of Archangel Michael and St Bishoy's Coptic Orthodox church in Sydney, Australia. He is extensively involved in theological education and service for high school and University youth.

Cover Design:
Mariana Hanna
In and Out Creation Pty Ltd
inandoutcreations.com.au

Text Layout:
Hani Ghaly,
Begoury Graphics
begourygraphics@gmail.com

CONTENTS

1. BEFORE YOU START

1. BEFORE YOU START

The Liturgy brings God, humanity and the world together... it's a mini incarnation... an incarnation of sound, smell, taste and touch. Salvation in the Orthodox church comes through union and intimacy with God, finding its greatest expression in the liturgy. The liturgy is the moment of unity between all of creation throughout all the ages – the point where past and future all come together into the present. The instant where heaven and earth are one – when God wraps His outstretched arms around His children who are seeking His embrace.

Sometimes the liturgy can get a bit confusing... even boring. We ask why this is the case and we often hear the same answer "You don't understand, when you understand then you will love it." The point of this book isn't to try and capture all the detailed descriptions and contemplations on the entire liturgy. If we tried to do that we could probably fill an entire library. Instead, the purpose of this book is to help those of us who sometimes struggle to connect with God and one another through the liturgy; to share just a few gems from the many that the liturgy has to offer. These gems will help us to understand why the liturgy is interesting to some people and what I am missing out on by not understanding it.

One of the greatest barriers for people is a misunderstanding of the nature and meaning of the activity in which we are participating. When you go around and ask people what the liturgy is, the most common response is "the time we eat the body and blood of Christ." Yet the significance of this is often lost on us. The act of eating is very intimate – after all, the typical romantic date for a couple is to go and have a meal together. Whenever there is a celebration, it is done over a meal. It is quite rare for someone to share a meal with a person they dislike – sharing a meal is considered a sign of intimacy.

As such, the sharing of the life-giving meal, the body and blood of Christ, is the most intimate sign of love, both between God and His children, and between His children among themselves. More than an ordinary meal, it is the only meal that truly satisfies.

When Adam and Eve fell, all of creation fell with them. Thus, death – the consequence of sin – was passed onto all of creation through them. Name one thing we eat that is not dead or dying? Every animal is dead before we eat it, every vegetable has been plucked or harvested from its life source and is dead before we eat it, and as they say, 'you are what you eat'. So if we are what we eat and all we are eating is dead, then are we not dead also?

But when we eat the body and blood of Christ, we eat food that is alive. Just as our Lord Jesus said, "I am the Resurrection and the Life" (John 11:25). So we are literally eating life, and in doing so we become alive – confirming the priest's proclamation

What the Fathers Say

We therefore ask that our Bread, which is Christ, be given to us daily, so that we who abide and live in Christ may not withdraw from His sanctification and from His Body.

– St Cyprian

What the Fathers Say

The Eucharist is the medicine of immortality, the antidote against death, and everlasting life in Jesus Christ.

– St. Ignatius of Antioch

during the liturgy that His body and blood gives "eternal life to those who partake of Him."

In the book of Revelation, Jesus says, "Behold, I stand at the door and knock. If anyone hears My voice and opens the door, I will come in to him and dine with him, and he with Me" (Revelation 3:20). This verse is basically saying He will enter into those people who are intimate with Him. They will become one through a dining experience. This is none other than the divine meal of holy communion – which takes place during the mystery of the liturgy.

WHY ARE YOU BORED?

How many times have you been in the liturgy and someone approaches you asking if the service is nearly finished? I remember one time during the liturgy a young boy, probably about four years old, tugged on my tunic and waved for me to bend down. I leaned in, the boy mumbled what I could only make out to be, "Whnbrdime?" Totally confused and not having a clue what he said I smiled at him and replied "yes, of course." He seemed pretty happy with the answer so I didn't think much of it. About 10 minutes later, he tugged on my tunic again and muttered, "whn bd time?" I still had no idea what he said, but I did pick up on one word… "time." So I leaned in and asked him to repeat what he said. He seemed quite annoyed at my inability to understand him, so he said much slower, "When is bread time?" Oh bread time! That's what he was saying! It took me a second or two to realise he was asking when holy communion was going to begin. The kid was clearly bored. I mean he is only a kid, it's perfectly understandable. Actually, when I thought about it, it was pretty cute. But when does it stop being understandable and cute? It may be acceptable for a child but what about a teen? Or an adult? How can we justify their boredom?

Imagine you were to watch a sport that you knew nothing about, say tennis. If you do not know the rules of a game, watching a three hour long match would be the most excruciating experience you would ever have. "So what is all the fuss about? Why do the players walk out of the field and walk back in?" And if it was a close game with extra sets, you would be justified to ask why a two hour game could just be extended to three

What the Fathers Say

Therefore run together as into one temple of God, as to one altar, as to one Jesus Christ, who came forth from one Father

– St. Ignatius of Antioch

The Liturgy

The word liturgy (Grk. leitourgia: "liow" meaning "people", and "ergia" meaning "work") is translated "work of the people", or "a public service undertaken on behalf of people". You cannot have a liturgy without at least one member of the congregation present. For it is, essentially, a public service!

People, Places &Things

What the Fathers Say

Recently I attended a liturgy at St Mary's church and Fr Bishoy Yassa, a very saintly elder priest was also praying. After he had communion he reclined himself on the floor behind the altar and continued praying the psalms. The liturgy is an enjoyable time spent in God's company and sometimes we just never want it to end

— Fr Mark Basily

hours? And most of all you might ask, "Why do people pay so much money to watch this?" All these questions would be justifiable if you did not know the rules of the game. But if you knew the rules of the game, a three hour game would be a short game because you would be able to follow and interact with the rules of the game. The same goes for the liturgy – if we put some effort to understand what is going on in the liturgy, it is really only a matter of time before you fall in love with it. It is understandable that those who don't know what is happening in the liturgy will get bored. That is why we need to put a lot of effort to learn what is happening, to try to enjoy and appreciate the fullness of the liturgy.

BUT JUST HOW AWESOME
CAN THE LITURGY BE?

There is a hymn sung in Swahili speaking Orthodox churches, just before the Liturgy of the Word, that says, "twendeni safari kulea binguni" which basically means, "let's go on an adventure ascending into heaven." That is such a great way to put it! The liturgy is an adventure that takes us to heaven, it is the uniting place between heaven and earth. But more than this, we ourselves become the dwelling place of God: our hearts become the throne of God when we eat His body and blood. As St John Chrysostom says, "But what do I care about heaven, when I myself have become heaven?"

How beautiful a thought, that we who partake of God have become heaven. What further proof do we need of God's humble love for us than this, that He is willing to take us to this elevated state? Yet even this is not the full picture. Not even this is the full extent of the grace, the undeserving gift, God has bestowed on us. Don't take my word for it, you need to experience it for yourself.

REFLECTION

Make a decision to find out as much as you can about the liturgy. The simplest way is to follow on from the book and read the instructions and priest's silent prayers. Take note of things that don't make sense and search in books or ask older deacons about the meaning.

LITURGICAL CYCLE

Daily Cycle	Weekly Cycle	Monthly Cycle	Yearly Cycle
Psalms prayers	The psalmody	29th of the Coptic Month (commemoration of Annunciation, Nativity and Resurrection)	The Lordly feasts (7 major & 7 minor)
Morning Raising of Incense	The day of crucifixion (Friday)	21st of the Coptic month (the monthly feast of St. Mary)	The feasts of St Mary
Evening Raising of Incense	The day of betrayal (Wednesday)	12th of the Coptic month (the monthly feast of Archangel Michael)	The feasts of the cross
	The day of Resurrection (Sunday)		The feast of Nayrouz
			The feasts of saints

LITURGICAL CYCLE

Before we begin, we should mention why the church has different seasons. For example, the reason why the church is joyful one day, and then mournful on another. Why the church colours change from red, to black and then to white all within the same week.

That is the nature of our church. There is constant change in the church season that can be easily noticed if we pay attention. The church is exciting and likes to mix things up every now and then by giving us seasons in the year. The church even breaks up the day to help us get in touch with Christ and the life He lived.

The cycle of liturgical prayer can be divided into four segments: daily, weekly, monthly and yearly cycles.

THE DAILY CYCLE (CANONICAL HOURS)

"Through the Lord's mercies we are not consumed, because His compassions fail not. They are new every morning; great is Your faithfulness." – Lamentations 3:22-23

- First Hour (Prime) (Morning Prayer)
- Third Hour (Terce)
- Sixth Hour (Sext)
- Ninth Hour (None)
- Eleventh Hour (Sunset Prayer)
- Twelfth Hour(Compline) (Prayer Before Sleeping)
- Midnight Prayer

The organisation of the Christian prayers begins with the vespers, morning and noontime prayers; that is, the beginning, the middle and end of the day. This is how Daniel the prophet prayed: "he [Daniel] knelt down on his knees three times that day, and prayed and gave thanks before his God, as was his custom since early days" (Daniel 6:10). The idea of consecrating time in each day for God has clear Hebrew origins.

Eventually, as Christianity developed its own identity and deviated from Judaism, the early church established its hourly liturgical cycle. Pliny the younger, a first century historian who was not a Christian believer himself, makes note of fixed times of prayer by Christians outside the liturgy of the Eucharist, specifying a morning prayer: "they met on a stated day before it was light, and addressed a form of prayer to Christ, as to a divinity..."

By the third century, the desert fathers and mothers began to live out the instruction of St Paul the apostle to "pray without ceasing" (1 Thessalonians 5:17). The monks and nuns would arrange for a group of them to pray one canonical hour and another group to pray the next hour, and thereby, as a community, they achieved prayer without ceasing.

The first hour (Prime) or the morning prayer is instituted to commemorate the hour at which Christ rose from the dead. "Now on the first day of the week, very early in the morning, they, and certain other women with them, came to the tomb bringing the spices which they had prepared." (Luke 24:1). In the first hour we also remember the incarnation of Christ. We acknowledge that He is the True Light and we ask Him to enlighten us.

The third hour (Terce) is instituted to commemorate the hour at which Christ was condemned. Also at this hour the Holy Spirit came down on the apostles. During the third hour the Holy Spirit descended upon the Holy Disciples and saintly apostles as "they were all with one accord in one place" (Acts 2:1). In the original Greek, the word "accord" translates to "harmony of sounds", and so there must have been deep, unified prayer by the believers present at that third hour.

The sixth hour (Sext) is instituted to commemorate the crucifixion of Christ. Also the bible says "Peter went up on the housetop to pray, at about the sixth hour" (Acts 10:9), thus there are allusions to prayer at the sixth hour having its roots from the apostles and earlier Jewish traditions.

The ninth hour (None) is instituted to commemorate the hour of the death of Christ in the flesh, and the right-hand thief who found favour in His eyes. One of the clearest pieces of evidence that the hourly liturgical cycle has Hebrew roots is found in the book of Acts: "Now Peter and John went up together to the temple at the hour of prayer, the ninth hour" (Acts 3:1). This suggests that there was a specified time people would aim to go and worship in the temple – at the ninth hour.

The eleventh hour or the sunset prayer is instituted to commemorate the time when the body of Christ was taken down from the cross, anointed and wrapped in linen.

The twelfth hour (Compline), or the prayer before sleeping, is instituted to commemorate the laying down of the body of our Lord Jesus Christ in the tomb. It is also the last hour of a believer's life in the day, as sleep is considered to be a mini-death. When we wake up from this mini-death, we rise up to pray the first hour prayer, which commemorates the resurrection. It implies that we too are made to rise from death, and are now risen with Christ in the first hour of the day. Thus, we die and rise daily.

Each day is an opportunity to repent having in mind our pending daily death and, if we are worthy, of our resurrection in the morning. "They [God's mercy and compassion] are new every morning"(Lamentations 3:23). This is very comforting, as to the Lord, every day is a clean slate! Every day is a new chance!

"Repeatedly, something in us has to die so that we may pass on the next stage of living. The transition from the baby to the child, from the child to the adolescent, from the adolescent to the mature adult, involves at each juncture an inner death in order that something new may come alive. And these transitions, particularly in the case of the child becoming a teenager, can often be crisis-ridden and even acutely painful. Yet if at any point we decline to accept the need for a dying, we cannot develop into real persons. Without the death there would be no new life." – Metropolitan Kallistos Ware

The midnight prayer is the time to remember judgement day – that Christ is coming when we least expect. It is also a reminder of when Christ went to Hades and preached to those who were there, saving each person who believed in Him, leading them to freedom and taking them to heaven. The gospels of this hour remind us of our judgement and final passing, which makes sense, given that at this point we are in mid-sleep (death).

WEEKLY CYCLE

The weekly cycle is a little simpler:

•   Monday, Tuesday and Thursday are normal seasonal days and have no real special significance.

•   Wednesday and Friday are the two days of the week that we were instructed by the apostles to fast (except the holy 50 days of resurrection). This is written in The Didache, an ancient document believed to be written by the apostles, that gives instructions on Christian life and how to run the church. "Let not your fasts be with the hypocrites, for they fast on Mondays and Thursdays, but you fast on Wednesdays and Fridays" (Didache 8.1).

•   Saturday is still the Jewish Sabbath and although we do not observe it the same way as the Jews do, we do acknowledge it as the allegorical day the Lord rested from creation. It also reminds us of Jesus being the completion of the Old Testament, and that old traditions have been replaced by unity with Christ.

•   Sunday is the day of the Lord. It is the weekly commemoration of the resurrection of Jesus our Messiah from the dead and the uniting of heaven and earth, God and man.

MONTHLY CYCLE

According to the Coptic (Alexandrian) calendar, the Coptic church celebrates and commemorates certain fasts, feasts, miracles, and lives of Saints on certain days of the year. For example:

On the 12th day of each Coptic month, the church commemorates Archangel Michael.

On the 21st day of each Coptic month, the church commemorates the Virgin and holy Theotokos St Mary.

On the 29th day of the Coptic month, the church commemorates the Annunciation of the Birth of Christ to St Mary, the Nativity of Christ and the Resurrection.

The effect these dates have on the liturgy often goes further than people realise. Not only are extra hymns sung, but usually the readings of that day are adapted to celebrate or commemorate that feast or saint. On one of the monthly feasts of Archangel Michael(12th Paone) certain extra hymns may be sung in each service, one of which is: "Through the Intercessions of the holy Archangel Michael, the chief of the heavenlies, O Lord grant us the forgiveness of our sins". Also, the readings on the feast of Archangel Michael are clearly related to his feast, they are:

The psalm of the Vespers – "Praise the Lord! Praise the Lord from the heavens; Praise Him in the heights! Praise Him, all His angels; Praise Him, all His hosts" (Psalm 148:1-2)

The psalm of the Matins; "Who makes His angels spirits, His ministers a flame of fire. Who makes the clouds His chariot, Who walks on the wings of the wind" (Psalm 104:4, 3)

The epistle of St Paul – "He says: Let all the angels of God worship Him. And of the angels He says: Who makes His angels spirits and His ministers a flame of fire" (Hebrews 1:6-7)

The catholic (universal) epistle – "Yet Michael the archangel, in contending with the devil, when he disputed about the body of Moses, dared not bring against him a reviling accusation, but said, The Lord rebuke you!" (Jude 1: 9)

And during the Fraction, the priest will pray the Fraction for "The feasts of the Virgin and the Angels".

So it is clear that the church magnifies the celebrations of the saints and feasts by commemorating them in the liturgy.

YEARLY CYCLE

The yearly cycle is as follows and is the main reason for changes of colour and tunes in the church.

Major Feasts:

1. Nativity
2. Epiphany
3. Palm Sunday
4. Resurrection
5. Ascension
6. Pentecost
7. Annunciation

Minor Feasts:

1. Circumcision
2. Wedding of Cana of Galilee
3. Entry of Christ into the Temple
4. Covenant Thursday
5. Thomas Sunday
6. Entry of Christ into Egypt
7. Transfiguration

Fasts (Excluding Wednesday and Friday):

1.   Nativity

2.   Epiphany Paramoun

3.   Jonah's Fast

4.   Lent

5.   Holy Week

6.   Apostles' Fast

7.   St Mary's Fast

So the next time you notice a change in your diet, or a change in the colour of the curtains, or a different tune or hymn being sung, know that it is due to this liturgical cycle of the church. And as you read this book, try to find out what cycle we are in at the moment! And this week when you go to church, try to spot any differences.

2. GET READY

2. GET READY

A GOOD BEGINNING IS HALF THE JOB DONE

Imagine going to the gym without preparing. I have been guilty of doing this many times. Before the session I neither ate enough food, drank enough water, slept well nor prepared mentally. I ended up walking around the gym doing nothing and wasting my time – I received zero benefit. It wasn't that the gym was bad or the machines weren't working, I just wasn't prepared for the task at hand. Now think about it, if one isn't going to benefit from an almost mindless activity as a gym session without appropriate preparation, then how can one expect to benefit from the total sensory experience of the liturgy without appropriate preparation?

Good preparation is a fundamental component to success in any field and of course the liturgy is no exception. The Jews in the Old Testament observed a strict preparation routine. Before the High Priest entered the Holy of Holies, the most sacred part of the temple, he would recite psalms 120-134, known as the Song of Ascents. Approaching the Holy of Holies was a very big deal and was done with great reverence and fear. With each fearful step up toward the altar he took he would shakily breathe deeply and recite one of these psalms.

We too should recite psalms and lift up our hearts as we approach the new temple, the church. When we approach the sanctuary we should prepare ourselves by reciting psalms such as psalm 121 ("I was glad when they said to me, 'Let us go into the house of the Lord...'") or psalm 83 ("How lovely is your tabernacle, O Lord of Hosts...").

What is most important is not that you say the psalms but that you reflect on where you are and what you are about to partake of – the use of the psalms is a great help in achieving this purpose. The psalms are simply a tool to help us lift up our hearts to God. Think of it like this: whenever we are sick we go to a doctor. When we want to become a better athlete, we ask the professional athletes who have mastered the sport. Likewise, when we come to pray, we should look to the experts of prayer, the 'professors' of lifting up their hearts to God, who have written down their experiences with God in the book of psalms.

I hated it when my parents had guests coming over! They would make me and my brother clean the whole house! They would clean the living room, the kitchen, the bedrooms, the shower, the garage and when they were in a good mood we even had to clean the car... the car! Just in case the guests wanted to move the conversation from the house to the back seat. I am sure many of you have had similar experiences. The amount of preparation for a simple guest was extensive to say the least.

But maybe this mad preparation scheme has trained us for something. If that is how we prepared for a guest into our homes, how

What the Fathers Say

There is another lady in our church who I always noticed arrives before the priest. No matter how early I arrive she is still there before me. One time I asked her, why do you come so early even before the priest? She replied "I don't like to miss the moment the priest opens the sanctuary curtain. It gives me the feeling that the windows of heaven are being opened for us.

– Fr Elijah Iskander

much more should we prepare before we have Christ enter inside our hearts?

HOW TO PREPARE

Even if we pray regularly we should always make the appropriate preparations. What does a professional tennis player do more regularly than play tennis? Nothing... yet a tennis player always eats correctly, mentally switches on and warms up with a few rallies before a game. Even more so, no matter how many liturgies we may have attended, preparation for the work of the liturgy is necessary before partaking, especially when what we have been doing before the liturgy is of a totally different nature.

A good practice for not just the liturgy but any prayer is to dedicate some time before your session to meet God in silence and to still your heart and mind and ready it for what is about to happen.

Before a regular morning liturgy, this may mean waking up a little earlier and praying the first hour or a few psalms, this way you are warming yourself up to prayer. You may also go through the readings of that liturgy, so you may be more readily inclined to the message of the liturgy for that day. Another great thing to do to prepare is to recite the Jesus prayer, "My Lord Jesus Christ, the Son of God, have mercy upon me the sinner" especially in the car while your parents are driving you to church. Reciting this prayer constantly calms

What the Fathers Say

Before you begin to pray, stand a while, sit for a while, or walk a little and try to steady your mind and turn it away from all worldly activities and objects. After this, think who He is to whom you turn in prayer, then recollect who you are; who it is who is about to start this invocation to Him in prayer

— St. Theophan the Recluse

your mind and settles your heart, preparing you to receive the Lord.

It is important to take your time and not rush, even if it means you do not finish all the prayers you said you would complete. It is more important to pray slowly and with all your being. Prayer is not reading the psalms or chanting some hymns. To give an exact definition of prayer would be impossible because prayer in its essence is a mystery! The concept of finite humans talking to an infinite God, speaking comprehensible words to an incomprehensible God, is a total mystery!

A few friends and I went to the the USA and visited the White House. We got to the front gate and lined up waiting to enter. From the front gate we could see various security checkpoints and we started questioning whether any of us may have accidentally brought something that may not be allowed in. Before we even had a chance to find out, we were pulled aside by security who asked to see our passes. "Our passes?" we said to

What the Fathers Say

Prayer can do all things, for it moves the Hand that manages the whole universe

– Pope Kyrillos VI

Keep the psalms and the psalms will keep you

– Pope Shenouda III

Who is the main celebrant?

The main celebrant, also known as the officiating/offering priest, is the priest who touches the body and blood during the liturgy. That is, he breaks the body during the fraction and all other sections in the service where the body or blood is to be broken, dipped, kissed or touched in any way. Every other priest serving in the liturgy will only say the sections where the body and blood do not need to be handled.

People, Places &Things

What the Fathers Say

Spend the day
in preparation
for your prayer
at night

– St Isaac
the Syrian

one another, "What passes?" It turned out that to just enter the White House, we needed to have given at least two months' notice of our arrival. We also needed to submit multiple forms, copies of our passports as well as current photo ID. All this just to enter the White House! Imagine if we wanted to speak to the President. But to speak to the King of kings, the Creator of the universe, all we need to do is simply sign in, "In the name of the Father, the Son and the Holy Spirit..." What a mystery prayer is!

To try and put it simply, prayer is a tool used to be in intimate communion with God. So to rush through your prayers is to completely miss the point. It's not about how many prayers we have recited but how many prayers have led us to God, otherwise we have just simply recited words. So to prepare for the liturgy properly, it is important that we pray properly.

REFLECTION

The church has put together aids to assist us in preparing for the liturgy. A list of psalms to recite on your way to church. Maybe you can memorise these psalms and recite them in the car on your way to the liturgy.

WHAT IS HAPPENING BEHIND THE CURTAINS

Just before the priest puts on his service garments he asks to be absolved or forgiven by any priest and all the deacons present. He then proceeds to bless his garments as well as those of the deacons in the name of the Holy Trinity. This is the most common blessing used in the church, "In the name of the Father, the Son and the Holy Spirit, the One God, Amen. Blessed be God the Father the Pantocrator [loosely translated, 'Almighty'] Amen. Blessed be the Only Begotten Son Jesus Christ our Lord Amen. Blessed be the Holy Spirit the Paraclete [Comforter] Amen. Glory and honour, honour and glory, to the All-Holy Trinity, the Father, the Son, and the Holy Spirit, Amen."

The use of this Trinitarian prayer is so common in our liturgical prayers. Belief in the Holy Trinity is the most fundamental pillar of Christian theology. If anyone were to say they were Christian but did not believe in the Trinity then they are not Christian at all. Simply because this is who God is and if I do not worship God as who He is then I am worshiping a different God.

Hence when the priest says this prayer, at each "Amen" we should likewise respond saying, "Amen" as an expression of our concurring belief in the Trinity – the Father, the Son and the Holy Spirit.

The deacons who are having their tunic blessed in the altar might notice that, if there is more than one priest, the priests are playing a game of hot potato with the hand cross with each priest gently patting their own chest indicating for the other priest to start the prayer. The reason behind these humble but sometime funny gestures is that the priest who starts this Trinatarian prayer becomes the main celebrant of the liturgy and therefore the priests humbly put each other before themselves for this great honour.

3. DRESSING FOR THE OCCASION

3. DRESSING FOR THE OCCASION

DRESSED IN HEAVENLY GARMENT

I have never seen a professional football player wearing a suit while playing, and I probably never will. That's because the right outfit needs to be worn for the right occasion; this also goes for the liturgy. There are various contemplations on why the priest and deacons put on their ritual garments. One reason is that the garments highlight the fact that we are about to partake of something that transcends this world. It is a great visualisation of heaven; it reminds us that during the liturgy we are not on earth but in heaven. When God ordered Moses to make the priestly garment for Aaron he said it should be made "for glory and for beauty" (Exodus 28:2). Therefore these garments represent God's heavenly glory expressed through beauty in his creation.

When you read the Book of Revelation, St John describes the throne of God and the priests around him this way: "Around the throne were twenty-four thrones, and on the thrones I saw twenty-four elders sitting, clothed in white robes; and they had crowns of gold on their heads" (Rev 4:4). This is a very similar scene to the liturgy with the priests and deacons dressed in white, the priests having crowns on their heads.

WE PRAY WITH ALL THE CREATION

Humanity represents all of creation. When we put on the liturgical vestments, tunics and head scarves, we are not only sanctifying ourselves but by extension all of creation. Jesus often used creation to bless us and do His work. In the story of the five loaves and the two fish, Jesus used existing creation, bread and fish. He could have easily created food from nothing but instead used what was offered to fill those present. There are more stories where Jesus used normal creation to perform miracles: turning water into wine, dirt and saliva to new eyes, water as a footpath, and various others. The church follows the same example. This is most clearly seen in the mysteries of the church; not only is humanity becoming sanctified, but through the mysteries, all of creation becomes sanctified. In baptism, water is sanctified. In chrismation, oil – the product of plants and vegetation – is sanctified. In the Eucharist, all crops and food become sanctified. Thus, when man as the head of creation is clothed in these pure and holy

For Glory and Honour

God ordered Moses to make special garments for Aaron, his brother, the Levites, and the priests to use at the time of service, "And you shall make holy garments for Aaron your brother, for glory and for beauty. So you shall speak to all who are gifted artisans, whom I have filled with the spirit of wisdom, that they may make Aaron's garments, to consecrate him, that he may minister to Me as priest" (Exodus 28:2-3).

People, Places &Things

What the Fathers Say

He took from among creation that which is bread, and gave thanks, saying, 'This is My Body.' The cup likewise, which is from among the creation to which we belong, He confessed to be His Blood

-St. Irenaeus, Bishop of Lyons

garments, it is not only us men who are being transformed into pure and holy beings, but all of creation is also transformed.

WHY DO I HAVE TO WEAR MY TUNIC?

Some young deacons ask why they have to wear their tunic every week? Can't I just attend with the congregation for a change?

As a deacon you are supposed to fulfil your role as one… as a deacon (a chanter or a reader) your responsibility is to serve the Lord in the capacity you are ordained for during every liturgy. Being ordained at a young age and not having a say in the matter should not excuse you from this service. I want you to imagine with me the twenty four priests who are standing around the throne saying, "I don't feel like wearing the crown today" or "The censer is too heavy, I don't feel like holding it, I will stand with the Cherubim and the Seraphim just for today." As we agreed, being in the liturgy is like standing in heaven before the throne of God. The deacon's role is to lead the congregation in singing, and they should not abandon their role nor forsake their call to serve God's people and His altar.

A question was once handed to Pope Shenouda III during one of his weekly Wednesday sermons. The question started with, "I was asked to be a priest but I rejected the call…" at the end of this first line Pope Shenouda stopped reading the rest of the question and folded the paper and firmly told the anonymous man off. He said, "God called you to His priesthood and you rejected it? The King of kings called you to serve Him and you said no? How can you reject the King of kings! How dare you reject God!"

A youth told a priest that wearing a tonya was uncool, and that it was just for the kids and old people. Abouna responded saying that we should never be too cool for God's service. If anything we should be very passionate and excited to serve as a deacon!

WHY WHITE

The church has chosen white as the colour for the service vestments, for the following reasons:

- It is mentioned about God Himself: "Who cover Yourself with light as with a garment" (Psalm 104:2). "And the Ancient of Days was seated; His garment was white as snow" (Daniel 7:9).

- In the Lord's Transfiguration before His Disciples: "He was transfigured before them. His face shone like the sun, and His clothes became as white as the light" (Matthew 17:2).

- The angels' garments when they appeared at the time of the Resurrection were white: "And she saw two angels in white sitting" (John 20:12).

- In the Book of Revelation, it is mentioned: "He who overcomes shall be clothed in white garments" (Revelation 3:5).

The white colour represents the concepts of purity, cleanliness, innocence, sanctification of the heart, and the virtues that God's ministers should have. "And to her it was granted to be arrayed in fine linen, clean and bright, for the fine linen is the righteous acts of the saints" (Revelation 19:8).

4. OFFERING OF THE LAMB

4. OFFERING OF THE LAMB

THE OFFERTORY

"Before the uncovering of the relics of St. Theodosius of Chernigov, the priest-monk who was conducting the re-vesting of the relics became weary while sitting by the relics, dozed off and saw before him the Saint, who told him: 'I thank you for laboring with me. I beg you also, when you serve the Liturgy, to commemorate my parents.' 'How can you, O Saint, ask my prayers, when you yourself stand at the heavenly Throne and grant to people God's mercy?' the priest-monk asked. 'Yes, that is true,' replied St. Theodosius, 'but the offering at the Liturgy is more powerful than my prayer.' – St. John of Shanghai and San Francisco

The main events in this section are:

- The washing of the priests hands.

- The selection and preparation of the loaf of bread that will become the Body of Christ.

- The procession of the Lamb.

CLEAN YOUR COUCH!

The first notable thing that happens in this section is that the priest washes his hands. The washing of the priest's hands isn't so much about hygiene as it is a symbol of the purification of his heart. Remember the words of Christ when He said in Matthew 23:26, "first cleanse the inside of the cup and dish, that the outside of them may be clean also." Jesus was referring to the cleansing of the heart as being of foremost importance, more than any outward or physical cleansing. In fact, in Mark 7:1-23, Jesus reveals how upset He is at the Jews for blindly following customs such as washing their hands, utensils, and even washing their couches – yep, their couches! Now I'm sure if your mum saw anyone wet her couch she would be really upset as well. However, Jesus wasn't concerned that people's couches may be damaged, but rather that they were performing these activities without paying attention to cleaning their inner life. Often, these outward practices were observed for vain reasons and out of a desire for the praise of others – that the Jews would have people calling them blessed and righteous.

What the Fathers Say

Wash me thoroughly from my iniquity, and cleanse me from my sin

– Psalm 51:2

Ritual washing of hands, as well as other physical practices, may seem a little odd to some people but going through the liturgy we will notice something very important. In the liturgy we commonly use physical activities to express spiritual realities. The washing of hands as spiritual cleansing, the use of incense as our prayers being lifted up to heaven, partaking of bread and wine as the body and blood of Christ and the list goes on. This is because we as human beings are physical as well as spiritual and intellectual. Christ not only redeemed and sanctified our spirits but also our bodies. So the church in her wisdom uses all of who we are to worship God.

These practices of worship aren't human inventions but are given to us directly from God. If we go back to the Old Testament we can see that God gave meticulous instructions to Moses on how He wanted to be worshipped. The first Christians who were mainly Jews were using these practices in their daily prayers and we continue to use them until today. The problem Jesus had when he was rebuking the Jewish priests for their practices was not the practices themselves but that they were practicing these physical activities as ends in themselves – forgetting the spiritual realties they reflect. So when we see the priest wash his hands, we need to take a moment and ask ourselves, if I have been regular in cleansing myself through regular repentance and confession. It's also a great

REFLECTION

We are invited to have all our sins washed away from us and to make a new start with God. It's the perfect time to pray to God to wash away my sins and keep me holy as he is holy. If I have been away from my confession father for a while, I should set a time to go and see him.

time to pray to God to cleanse our hearts and to take away the sins that keep me away from Him.

ONLY OFFER THE BEST

After the priest washes his hands he goes to the door of the altar and finds the deacons carrying the wine, water and the basket containing the loaves of bread all waiting for him.

The priest proceeds to do the sign of the cross on himself and prays the trinitarian prayer, blessing in the name of the Father, the Son and the Holy Spirit, showing that the Trinity is the focus of our worship.

He will then pick up the wine and smell it to judge whether the wine is good or bad, passing it around to the other altar deacons to confirm. If one thinks the wine is good they are to say "right and worthy", but if they think it is bad then the wine is replaced and the testing process begins again.

This testing has an important practical side as no one wants to drink bad wine, but it also has a significant spiritual meaning. We should only be offering God the best of our gifts. When God wanted to offer us something He offered us none other than Himself. If you remember the story of Cain and Abel (Genesis 4:1-15), God looked at Abel's sacrifice and accepted it with joy as Abel offered the Lord from the best of what he had; the first born of his flock. Whereas Cain offered to the Lord

What the Fathers Say

If you cannot find Christ in the beggar at the church door, you will not find Him in the chalice

– St John Chrysostom

What the Fathers Say

He who clothes the whole world with its varied beauty, is wrapped up in common linen, that we might be able to receive the best robe; He by Whom all things are made, is folded both hands and feet, that our hands might be raised up for every good work, and our feet directed in the way of peace

– Ambros of Milan

from the remains of what he had, and God wasn't very impressed with his offering.

CHOOSING THE OFFERING

Next, the priest begins to examine the loaves of bread to choose the most suitable one for the offering. This offering must be perfect and "without blemish" just as Exodus 12:5 describes the Passover lamb; the Passover lamb in the Old Testament points to Christ in the New. Both the Passover lamb and the bread offered in the liturgy represent Christ who out of all humanity was the perfect man.

Having selected the lamb, the priest pulls out a decorated cloth and wraps the selected lamb. This cloth symbolises both the swaddling clothes in the manger and the burial shrouds in the tomb – a symbol of both His birth and His death.

THE BABY BORN TO DIE

The priest begins examining the loaves presented to select the most perfect one to become the body of Christ and he cries out, "O Lamb of God who takes away the sins of the world, hear us and have mercy upon us!" It is to this gentle and pure lamb, the image of the baby Jesus, that we look for our victory and salvation. Thus we respond by crying "Kyrie Eleison (Lord have mercy)", 41 times, remembering the suffering and pain this innocent lamb is destined to go through because of His great love for us.

In Luke 2:9, we hear that the baby Jesus was wrapped in swaddling clothes. Now most of us may read this and just assume that swaddling clothes are the typical baby wrapping material. However, there is actually something far deeper unfolding right before our eyes, highlighted in this section of the liturgy – when the priest wraps the selected loaf with a cloth. Some scholars say swaddling clothes are what poorer elderly men carried around with them just in case they died on a journey, or were unable to be buried in a tomb. So should an elderly man die on a journey they would thus be wrapped in these swaddling clothes and their bodies were somewhat preserved. We often forget that St Joseph the carpenter, the earthly father of Jesus, was a rather elderly man at the time of the birth of Jesus. Thus the swaddling clothes the baby Jesus was wrapped in may have belonged to St Joseph; perhaps he used to carry these around just in case he died suddenly. It is a prophecy that this baby was to live a poor life and die a brutal death. The same way St Mary wrapped her baby Son was the same way Christ was wrapped before His burial. This is why when the angel appeared to the shepherds in Luke 2:12 we see the angel explain that the sign to find the One they should go and worship will be "a Babe wrapped in swaddling clothes, lying in a manger." It seems this was not a common sight at all. This was their sign - that they would find a baby wrapped in His grave clothes.

What the Fathers Say

Cast your burden on the Lord, And He shall sustain you; He shall never permit the righteous to be moved

– Psalm 55:22

What the Fathers Say

casting all your care upon Him, for He cares for you

- 1 Peter 5:7

So when we sing 'Lord have mercy', we must understand the scene that is unfolding before our eyes. That for our sake, God became an innocent Baby condemned to die in our shame, so we may live in His glory.

INSCRIBED IN CHRIST

Now, something rather moving begins to happen; it is often completely unnoticed. As the priest selects the lamb and wipes it down with the cloth, his eyes search the whole church and he begins to ask the Lord to bless each member in front of him by name, "remember O Lord Fr so and so, remember O Lord Verona, Remember O Lord Tim, Remember O Lord Michael, Remember O Lord Mark, Remember O Lord each member of your congregation."

How heart-warming is this moment? The priest asks Christ to remember you by name! As though he is entrusting us to God. All your pains and burdens, all your troubles and sorrows, all your confusion and anxiety are being cast onto the Lord. As though all these things are no longer on us, but are now God's responsibility. This happens just as the priest is about to anoint the Lamb with the wine – soon to be the blood. It really brings to life the verse, "I have inscribed you on the palms of My hands; Your walls are continually before Me" (Isaiah 49:16). We are literally being inscribed into this lamb, and all our problems, and the walls in our lives, are being placed before Christ.

It is a great time to remember to pray for others during this part of the liturgy. Ask the Lord to also bless those in your life who are going through a difficult time or making a big decsision in their life. It is good to remember your loved ones and everyone in your life. It is also a good time to remember those who are making your life hard – your enemies and those who are against you. Gather all of these and put them onto the Lord, and He will take care of everything.

The sacrifice of Melchizedek

Once wiped down with the cloth, the priest touches the unselected loaves in the basket with the selected one, emphasising that all the sacrifices of the Old Testament point to this lamb, Jesus, and His sacrifice on the cross, as He was the fulfilment of all these

REFLECTION

Pain and love. When we live our life and pain comes our way don't be surprised... it is through this pain that love is born, grown, shaped and eternalised. So put your pain on the altar, on this lamb who not only takes away the sin of the world, but also transforms your pain and burdens into blessings beyond whatever you can imagine, the greatest of which is love

What the Fathers Say

The Lord has sworn And will not relent, 'You are a priest forever According to the order of Melchizedek'"

- Psalm 110:4

This Melchizedek was at the same time both priest and king; he was to be a type of Christ, and Scripture makes clear mention of this

- St. John Chrysostom

sacrifices. The priest then anoints the selected loaf with the wine and says, "Sacrifice of glory", then crosses the unselected loaves saying, "Sacrifice of blessing, Sacrifice of Abraham, Sacrifice of Isaac, Sacrifice of Jacob." The priest then does something a little strange; he returns to the chosen lamb and blesses it again saying "Sacrifice of Melchizedek."

But who is Melchizedek? And why is the chosen lamb, the one to become the Body of Christ, said to be a sacrifice of Melchizedek? While the loaves that weren't chosen, sacrifices of other prominent biblical figures? Is this Melchizedek greater than Abraham, Isaac and Jacob?

To answer this, we need to look at Genesis 14. In that passage, foreign kings had kidnapped Lot, Abraham's nephew. Abraham being the great uncle he was, went with a small band of his men – 318 to be exact – to rescue Lot. After the rescue, a man by the name of Melchizedek, who was both "priest of God Most-High" and "king of Salem" brings out bread and wine and puts his hands on Abraham and blesses him.

Don't worry, I know what you're thinking, "There were offerings of bread and wine in the Old Testament? Melchizedek, some random guy who pops up out of nowhere, blesses Abraham the great man of faith? What is going on?"

Well, to get more perspective, let's read Hebrews 7:7, "Now beyond all contradiction the lesser [Abraham] is blessed by the better [Melchizedek]." So it seems that this high priest Melchizedek is "better", as St Paul says, than Abraham. This is where it may get a bit technical. Now from the seed of Abraham arises the Jewish priestly tribe called the tribe of Levi. The Levites were the priests who performed all the Old Testament sacrifices. So this passage tells us that the priesthood of Melchizedek is "better" than the priesthood of the Old Testament Levites. Thus the sacrifice of Melchizedek, bread and wine, is greater than all of the Levitical Old Testament sacrifices!

This is seen in the last supper where Jesus uses bread and wine for His body and blood rather than a lamb, dove or any other Old Testament offering. And it is seen in this moment right now in the liturgy. The sacrifice of sacrifices is to be offered on the altar before our very eyes, in the form of bread and wine.

That is why Melchizedek is given such honour. His offering is a prophecy of the New Testament offering of bread and wine, the body and blood of Christ. Thus, Melchizedek's priesthood is superior to the entire Old Testament priesthood because his sacrifice is a type of the greatest sacrifice of all - Jesus Christ, the Lamb of God.

What the Fathers Say

You are a priest forever, according to the order of Melchizedek.' He did not say: 'According to the order of Aaron

– St. John Chrysostom

PRIESTHOOD OF AARON AND MELCHIZEDEK

Although the priesthood of Aaron in the Old Testament was established by God for the people to offer sacrifices for the forgiveness of sins, it was not sufficient to save the whole world. It was only through Christ's offering on the Cross –the true lamb of God – that the whole world is saved from death and sin. After Jesus' sacrifice on the cross all the Old Testament sacrifices are made redundant and therefore the Old Testament priesthood is of no effect. Now we have the priesthood of Christ or of Melchizedek, a type of Christ.

What is typology – what does being a "type of Christ" mean?

A type in scripture is a person or thing in the Old Testament which foreshadows a person or thing in the New Testament. For example, the flood in the time of Noah in Genesis 6-7 is used as a type of baptism in 1 Peter 3:20-21.

INCARNATION AND DEATH

Now the majority of symbolism in the liturgy can be classified into two main categories. The first is symbolism relating to the incarnation. The second is symbolism relating to the death and resurrection.

At this point, all the other loaves are blessed by being touched by the Lamb, for Christ blessed human nature when He touched it through His incarnation. The lamb and the other loaves are then anointed with wine in the shape of a cross. The wine represents blood which symbolises both life and death. Christ came to earth and shared our life by becoming fully human, yet He took our shame upon Himself and died the death we deserve and through the shedding of His blood we have eternal life. In the incarnation, Christ became 'one blood' with us, taking on our human nature in body and blood. With his death, Christ having taken on all of humanity into Himself, offers Himself on the cross, conquering death on behalf of all.

The priest having returned to the altar with all the altar servants, washes the lamb very similarly to how a midwife washes a newborn baby. This brings to mind that Jesus came into the world both full God and fully man, to the point of humbling Himself to become a newborn baby washed and wrapped in clothes. The Almighty God who clothed the sky with stars humbled Himself to the point that He was too helpless to even clothe Himself.

THE LAMB IN THE CLOTH

Here the procession of the Lamb takes place. It is an interesting scene, the priest carries the lamb wrapped in a cloth to his head and places a cross on top. He then processes around the altar with deacons following behind him chanting. There are various symbolic references in this scene.

What the Fathers Say

The bread and wine resemble us that we are an oblation to God. As the bread cannot be offered before going through many phases, so likewise we must pass with our Lord through the fire of His suffering. Also as the wine is not offered before it is pressed, we must be pressed with Him through the winepress of His Cross, so that we may be offered to Him

– Fr Tadros Yacoub Malaty

One of these symbols is the biblical reference to Luke 2 when Joseph and Mary present Him to the temple and Simeon lifts up the baby Jesus and professes Him to be the Messiah. It is also symbolic of Christ carrying His cross as He walked through Jerusalem (the altar) to Golgotha, the place where He was crucified, which was done for the "peace and edification" of the church as mentioned at this point in time by the priest "peace and edification to the one, only, holy, catholic, and apostolic church of God..." Another example is the washing and wrapping of the lamb, which is symbolic of the dead body of Christ. When the lamb is washed and shrouded for burial, it is carried by the priest with honour above his head, facing the people. After this prayer it is gently placed in the paten as Joseph of Arimathea and Nicodemus gently placed Christ's body in the tomb.

EARLY CHURCH SAYINGS OF THE FATHERS

The Didache, an ancient Christian document that includes instructions believed to be written by the Apostles and their direct disciples, states that as bread is made up from many grains and wine from many grapes, so too is Christ, who is the Head of His Body. We are all the grains and grapes, united as one in the bread and wine – the Body and Blood of Jesus.

St Cyprian, an early church Father says, "When the Lord calls bread, which is combined by the union of many grains, His Body and He indicates that our people whom He bore are as being united into one. And when He calls the wine, which is pressed from many grapes, His Blood, He also signifies that His flock are linked together by the mingling of a multitude into one."

REFLECTION

What do these symbols mean to me? It is a different message for everyone everyday. A prayer that you can pray here is, "Lord, as you entered the temple, as you entered the mount of Golgotha and as you entered the tomb, enter into my heart today. Enter into the temple of my body, immerse yourself into the waters of my being, climb over the mountains that are blocking You and enter into the darkest tomb of my heart. And as you conquered in all, conquer in me also.

THE BASKET THE BREAD AND ITS PATTERNS

BASKET

The basket holding the bread was originally made of hay, straw or other natural materials. This symbolises how Christ came to earth born in a simple manger. He likewise comes to us on the altar in a similar manner through the humble beginnings of the hay manger of the basket.

BREAD

The bread is usually chosen from a selection of three, five or seven loaves. The bread is very intricate in its design. It is round in shape, has one larger cross in the exact centre called the Spadikon, which is a symbol of Jesus. In fact "spadikon" is a Greek word which means "the Lord" or "Master". There are twelve smaller crosses around the spadikon; three at the top, three at the bottom, three on the right and three on the left, which are representative of the twelve apostles. It also has five holes in it which represent the five piercings of Jesus which are: the three nails (two hands and one for the feet) located directly to the right of the spadikon; one for the crown of thorns, located at the top left corner of the spadikon; and one for the piercing of the spear which was plunged into His side, situated at the bottom left of the spadikon. It also has the Greek words written around it that say, "Holy God, Holy Mighty, Holy Immortal".

There are certain criteria that need to be met. The loaf must:

- Be the best in appearance and roundness

- Have a clear Despotikon/Spadikon (the square cross in the middle of the loaf)

- Have the right number of pierced holes (five holes)

- Not have anything stuck to it

- Not have cracks.

5. LITURGY OF THE WORD

5. LITURGY OF THE WORD

LITURGY OF THE WORD

Not reading your bible is like spiritual smoking. You may not realise the damage from day to day but looking back you will notice you have been killing yourself! You will have developed spiritual emphysema so that you no longer have the breath to pray, you have ruined your eyes so that you can no longer see the ways of God, and you have serious heart conditions so that yours no longer beats with the Lord's.

But eating your daily spiritual bread through the reading of Scripture also kills you. It kills your breath so that the Holy Spirit breathes in you. It kills your vision so that you no longer see through your own eyes but through the eyes of God. And it kills your heart of stone and gives you a heart for love alone.

Reading your bible daily kills you, allowing Christ to live in you eternally. Not reading kills you, leading to eternal condemnation.

Either way you die, but only one of these deaths leads to a resurrection...

The Coptic church has a deep history of being the voice of Christianity when it comes to interpreting the bible. Great Coptic saints such as Athanasius, Cyril, Didymus the Blind and Origen were looked to by the world for their interpertation of the divinely inspired teaching of Scripture. The bible plays a very central role in the Coptic church and always has since the beginning of the great see of Alexandria, with our founder St Mark being an author of one of the four gospel accounts. The church takes great pride in the bible. This is manifest most in the daily readings of the liturgy– collectively known as The Liturgy of the Word.

> The Liturgy of the Word contains 5 clear readings from:
>
> - The Pauline: A letter of St Paul
> - The Catholicon: A letter from an author other than St Paul
> - Acts: The book of Acts
> - Synaxarion: The life of the saints of that day
> - The Gospel: A psalm and a gospel reading

There are also various offerings of incense during this time as well as numerous silent prayers prayed by the priest.

CIRCUIT OF INCENSE

The rubrics for this section are rather wordy but as with everything in the liturgy, there is a lot of symbolism attached to it. However, going over every detail is beyond our scope, so let's try and keep it simple.

To begin the circuit of incense, the priest will place five spoons of incense into the censer. He will then silently pray the prayer of the Pauline Epistle and begin the incense procession around the altar.

The priest begins by standing between

What the Fathers Say

We need not only read Sacred Scripture, but learn it as well and grow up in it. Realise that nothing is written in Scripture unnecessarily. Not to read Sacred Scripture is a great evil

– St Basil the great

Then another angel, having a golden censer, came and stood at the altar. He was given much incense, that he should offer it with the prayers of all the saints upon the golden altar which was before the throne. And the smoke of the incense, with the prayers of the saints, ascended before God from the angel's hand

- Revelation 8:3-5

the people and the altar and with the censer in his hand he completes 6 semi-circles (or 3 full circles) around the altar. The priest at this point is silently praying the 3 great litanies – the litany for: the Peace of the church, the Pope & Bishop, and for the People. A good way to remember this is the three P's – Peace, Pope, People. The deacons holding the cross and bible are on opposite sides of the priest praying the responses to these litanies as they also process around the altar.

The priest then goes outside of the altar and continues the incense circuit around the rest of the church, collecting the prayers and confessions of the people and offering it up to the Lord with the ascending sweet smelling incense.

There is one action that the priest does here that relates very nicely to the upcoming first reading from St Paul which can very easily be missed. As the priest is on his circuit, he stops before the altar, below the cross of the iconostasis and says silently, "This is He who offered Himself as an acceptable sacrifice, on the cross for the salvation of our race. His good Father smelled Him in the evening on Golgotha. He opened the doors of Paradise and restored us to our original rank. Through His Cross and His Holy Resurrection He restored mankind once again to the Paradise."

This is a beautiful moment. The scene of the incense ascending from under the cross up to heaven, just as the aroma of the sacrifice of Christ on the cross arose to heaven and was accepted by the Father, the same loving sacrifice is happening live right in front of our eyes, as if we were standing on the mount of Golgotha 2000 years ago. This entire scene is the underlying message of the letters of St Paul – the message of sacrificial love, the message of cruciformity.

Overall, the priest will have done a total of seven circles around the altar and church. This is like the people of Israel who circled the walls of Jericho seven times so that the walls of the evil city would fall down. Likewise, we do the same so that the walls of evil that obstruct the church and its people may also fall down. That the walls around our hearts may fall so that "the King of Glory may come in" (Psalm 24:9). That nothing may block the words about to be read from entering our hearts.

CENSING TO SAINTS

The most common hymn sung at this time is the 'hymn of intercessions'; beginning

What the Fathers Say

It is impossible to represent and to think of the cross without love. Where the cross is, there is love; in the church you see crosses everywhere and upon everything, in order that everything should remind you that you are in the temple of the God of love, the temple of love itself, crucified for us

– St John of Kronstadt

Gospel and Cross

The deacons processing around the altar with the priest during the circuit of incense hold the cross and in some churches the cross and the gospel

People, Places &Things

What the Fathers Say

For from the rising of the sun even to its setting, My name will be great among the nations, and in every place incense is going to be offered to My name, and a grain offering that is pure; for My name will be great among the nations,' says the LORD of hosts

- Malachi 1:11

with the Theotokos St Mary, then the heavenly hosts who rejoiced at His birth, and then all those who lived in the light of the Incarnation. Traditionally, the hymn of intercessions was just sung to St Mary and repeated three times, however, over time, we have added multiple saints.

The intercession of the saints is not usually seen by many as significant. However, the meaning of this section, if understood correctly, is really beautiful. It is in fact a key principle of Christianity. We are pleading that God forgives our sins through the intercessions and prayers of these saints. Not only for ourselves, but for the whole church – those alive in it now, those who are to come and those who have already come. Further, not just for the forgiveness of the sins of the Christians but also for those of the whole world. This is fundamental Christianity, that we pray for our loved ones, our enemies and the rest of the world.

BUT WHY BOTHER WITH THE SAINTS?

So why is there such a focus on saints? What is the point? Why are there even icons in the church?

If one was to walk into a home, they would often find photos of family members: immediate family, aunts, uncles, cousins and grandparents. Often these photos tell a story; the time that you went on a family vacation, the day your parents got married, your siblings' first ever school photos. It's not even uncommon for one to find photos of deceased family members – photos that tell a story. Because these people are dead, do you throw out the photos? Because you no longer see them, do you remove them from your home, as though they never had any significance to you? As though nothing can be learned from the stories told in these photos? The same is the case with the icons in church, these are our family photos – our family the church. We look at them and remember the time our great grandfather Mark introduced us to his Bridegroom, Christ. The time our grandmother Mary of Egypt returned to the church after a very long and repentant journey. The time our father Anthony risked it all and began the new venture of monasticism, attracting male and female disciples throughout history. The time our brothers Mina and George gave up their lives and remained faithful to our beloved One. The time our sister Demiana took 40 of our cousins on the heavenly adventure of a lifetime – destination, home!

How can we not appreciate this moment when looking at the icons this way? Obviously, the focus of the liturgy is on communing with the Holy Trinity. Praising the saints does not take away from that, because we don't praise them for themselves but for their example in achieving the goals we all aspire to achive, uniting with God. The biblical analogy that the church prefers to use is the body of Christ. Christ is the head of this body and we are the members so to neglect mentioning the saints is to neglect important members of this body.

What the Fathers Say

May my prayer be counted as incense before You; The lifting up of my hands as the evening offering

– Psalm 141:2

The second reason is that they are a reminder. It is easy to notice that icons are often found all over the church – on the walls, the roof, in the altar – however, none are found on the floor. Of course there is the notion of not placing icons on the floor out of respect, but it goes much deeper than that. As the priest raises prayers before these icons on the roof and walls, we notice that the only thing on the floor is...us. We are the icons on the floor! We are the icons that offer prayers on behalf of each other! We are the icons that are told to "go forth and make disciples of all nations" (Matthew 28:19). We are the icons that project the light of God to the whole world. We are the icons who are called to make our lives in the likeness of God, so that the world may see our lives and rejoice because in us they see the Light – in us they see God. We are the saints on the floor who are to "let our light so shine before men that they may see our good works and glorify our Father in heaven" (Matthew 5:16). When we walk into the church we have icons of the saints lining our path to the altar – on the left hand and on the right. They are guiding and leading us to the altar, pointing toward Christ who is present on the altar, pleading with us to pay attention to Him so we may partake as they partook. And as we return from the altar, having partaken of the body and blood of God, we look up at these saints, who by their example guide our path and show us how to bring to whole word Him with whom we have become one on the altar – just as they did.

WHAT IS THE CENSER AND INCENSE?

The incense is a physical representation of our prayers ascending toward God. We also raise incense before the icons of the saints asking them to carry our prayers to the throne of God on our behalf. The use of the censer is rooted in Jewish liturgical practices. The offering of incense is seen all over the Old Testament. We know that incense is also used in the book of Revelation, "Now when He had taken the scroll, the four living creatures and the twenty- four elders fell down before the Lamb, each having a harp, and golden bowls full of incense, which are the prayers of the saints" (Revelation 5:8).

The censer holds much symbolism. The censer can be seen as a symbol of St Mary who carried the Lord in her womb. The live coal (divinity) does not burn or harm the

Public Confessions!

There is a point at the end of the priest's incense route where he will stop before the altar and say "O Lord who accepted the confession of the thief on the cross, accept the confessions of your people." In the early church, this was the point at which the people would get up before the rest of the congregation and publicly confess their sins. However, the church in its wisdom decided to go for the more discrete method of having people confess their sins privately in the presence of a priest... good move!

People, Places &Things

bowl (the womb of St Mary). The three chains on the censor are a symbol of the Holy Trinity. Christ incarnated to offer Himself as a sweet smelling sacrifice at the altar, and the resultant aroma is a sacrifice for all of humanity, pervading throughout the whole church.

Another reason we have the censer and incense is because the smell of the incense is beautiful. The liturgy engages all of our senses; the sense of smell is no exception. Many who enter a church are at first struck by its sweet smell. It is often heard that church members are put at ease and comforted once they smell the incense as it reminds them of God and their communion with Him in the liturgy.

THE CATHOLIC EPISTLE, THE ACTS AND THE SYNAXARION

Before the hymn "Hail to you, O Mary", an epistle from St James, St Peter, St John or St Jude is read; these readings are known as the catholic or universal epistles. The priest will begin the same incense route as the Pauline Epistle, however, he will not leave the altar until the conclusion of the catholic epistle and the start of the reading from Acts. The symbolism behind this is that the apostles for a time only preached in Jerusalem and the altar represents Jerusalem. As a re-enactment of the preaching of the Apostles, the priest only raises incense inside the altar. Once the reading of the Acts begins, the priest then begins to raise incense outside the altar, a symbol of bringing the message of the gospel to those outside of Jerusalem. This happens because the gospel was not spread to the whole world until the time recorded in the book of Acts.

It is also good to mention here that on regular weekdays when there is no special liturgical season all the readings of the church are centred on the saint of the day mentioned in the Synaxarion. For example, during the feast of a prophet, the readings will be centred on prophets and their message: the Gospel reading has Jesus condemning the Jews for their ungodly ways and their killing for the prophets. Similarly, if the Synaxarion is a female saint then the Pauline, the Catholicon and the Acts would be read about the role of women in the church, and the gospel would be about the wise and foolish vigins, and the same goes for other categories of saints such as martyrs, bishops, monks, etc. This only applies to weekday liturgies during the yearly season; so Sunday liturgies don't follow this pattern.

The location of the reading of the Synaxarion after the Epistles and Acts readings is very meaningful. It is like the church is saying in the Epistles and Acts, "this is how you should live your life", and in the Synaxarion, "here is an example of someone who lived a life according to the readings".

It is also important to note here that

> **What the Fathers Say**
>
> The Holy Scriptures are our letters from home
>
> — Augustine of Hippo

the book of Acts which tells the story of the spread of the church all over the world does not end with the word "Amen", unlike all the other books of the New Testament. This is because the work of the spread of the message of the gospel is still taking place until today and until the end of time. Reading the Synaxarion after the book of Acts is a witness to the continuation of the spread of the gospel through the lives of these saints.

GOSPEL READING: DID NOT OUR HEARTS BURN

Many seem to have the impression that partaking of the Body and Blood of Christ is all that is necessary, with no build-up or preparation required – that one can attend after the gospel and still partake and benefit fully. That the first half of the liturgy "isn't that important". However, the church disagrees. If we read Luke 24, the story of the two disciples on the road to Emmaus after the death of Jesus, we see the faith of the two disciples shaken and confused. They knew Christ had died, but were unaware that He had just risen despite the proclamation by the women that Jesus was alive again. So as the two walked back home, having lost hope that Jesus was the Messiah, Jesus appeared to them, yet they were unaware that it was Jesus because their eyes were "restrained" probably due to their own unbelief. After the two disciples told Jesus all that had just happened in Jerusalem concerning Him, Jesus explains to them all the writings and prophecies concerning the

Christ, that everything the two were speaking about were actually indicators that Jesus was in fact the Messiah.

"And beginning at Moses and all the Prophets, He expounded to them in all the Scriptures the things concerning Himself" (Luke 24:27).

Yet despite this explanation by words, the two did not believe, nor were they able to see that it was Jesus who was in front of them. The three then sat down for a meal, and Jesus "took bread, blessed and broke it, and gave it to them. Then their eyes were opened and they knew Him" (Luke 24:31).

How amazing is this story! It later says that the two disciples looked at each other and agreed, "Did not our hearts burn within us while He talked with us on the road, and while He opened the Scriptures to us." (Luke 24:32). It is as if the two disciples said that the words He was speaking to them were screaming out "Jesus is the Messiah!" And these words became undeniable at the breaking of bread (Holy Communion).

So what is the point of mentioning this story? Well, just as Christ needed to explain the Scriptures before breaking the bread, which is Holy Communion, likewise we must attend the Liturgy of the Word and most importantly, the gospel, before partaking of the Body and Blood of Jesus. Christ Himself did not skip any steps in what I like to call "the walking liturgy of Emmaus". Neither can we say that one section of the liturgy is more important than another; for all are part of the same experience. But what if you don't understand the Liturgy of the Word? Or what if you feel you don't benefit? Well it seems these two disciples were in that exact position, but deep down they experienced a much deeper sensation: their "hearts burned within them", even though they weren't really aware of it. This burning softens the heart, melts it and prepares it for the partaking of the Body and Blood of Christ. So that when the joyful moment comes that we should partake of the mysteries, with our now softened and burning hearts (through the Liturgy of the Word), our eyes may be opened and we may know God (through the Liturgy of the Faithful)! It is the Liturgy of the Word that awakens us for the breaking of bread and the breaking of bread that gives meaning to the Liturgy of the Word.

WHAT'S OUR FOCUS

As mentioned, the Liturgy of the Word is the section in the liturgy that is focused on reading, hearing and contemplating on the word of God. In the Liturgy of the Faithful (to be explained in another chapter), we meet with the physical Word (Jesus) through His presence in the consecrated bread and wine. In the Liturgy of the Word, we meet with the Word of God (Jesus) through the Bible. Something cool to notice in the next liturgy: when you look at the right side of the altar during the Liturgy of the Word, you should see the decoratively encased bible (containing the New Testament and the Psalms) standing on display. This is because the focus of this section is on the word of God. However, once the Liturgy of the Faithful begins, that decoratively encased bible is moved to behind the throne where the chalice is kept, highlighting that the focus is no longer on the words of Christ but on His Body and Blood.

EARLY CHURCH - THE LITURGY OF THE CATECHUMENS

The Liturgy of the Word is also known as the Liturgy of the Catechumens. The title Liturgy of the Catechumens comes from the old practice where those who were 'studying' to become Christians ("catechumens") would attend this section only, and then leave at its end – before the recitation of the creed. This

REFLECTION

An effective suggestion given to me some time ago was to pre-read the readings the day before the liturgy. Contemplate on the message so that when you hear it in the Liturgy of the Word, it takes root in your heart and grows to yield fruit worthy of the message received.

was also supposed to apply for anyone who was not having communion, such as those who were under penance etc. Thus, only those who were having communion would be left to pray and partake in the Liturgy of the Faithful. It is through understanding and living the Liturgy of the Word that the new Christian, and any Christian for that matter, approaches the Liturgy of the Faithful.

The early church considered the Eucharist to be a profound and great mystery, not something for those who could not yet understand and appreciate it. They paid heed to St Paul's warning that the one who partakes of the Lord's Body and Blood in an "unworthy manner" would bring condemnation upon themselves. Thus, it was not out of a sense of superiority over others that they excluded anyone who was ill-equipped for the Eucharist, but out of compassion for their souls. A catechumen should be educated first, and then joyfully baptised and admitted

People, Places &Things

Who are the Catechumens?

Catechumens are people who want to be baptised in Christ and His church, who want to be part of the Body of Christ. What usually happens is that they express their interest in the church; the church will then place them under the supervision of godparents who should instruct them and bring them up in the faith, educating and teaching them about Christ and the faith. When they are ready, they are baptised and become part of the body of Christ.

to this great mystery. A penitent should repent first, then be absolved and admitted back to this great mystery.

TRISAGION HYMN

The hymn "Agios" is one of the oldest and most well-known hymns in all of Christianity, both in the Coptic and all other traditional churches. It is sung in Greek in every traditional church, even the Latin Roman Catholic church sings it in Greek, which is really saying something. Don't forget Christianity was preached to most of the world in Greek since, during the first few centuries, it was the dominant world language.

Tradition tells us that on the way to the tomb to bury Jesus, Joseph and Nicodemus began to doubt that Jesus was really God. At that moment they heard angels singing "Holy God, Holy Mighty, Holy Immortal". Their doubts were immediately abolished and they began to sing with the angels. Later on they added the line, "who was crucified for us, have mercy upon us."

CIRCUIT OF INCENSE

Two deacons stand on the eastern side of the altar facing west, holding the Cross and Gospel. They proceed around the circuit saying:

1. Pray for the Peace of the One, Holy, Catholic and Apostolic Orthodox Church of God

2. Pray for our High Priest, Pope Abba ___, Pope, Patriarch and Archbishop of the great city of Alexandria, and for his partner in the apostolic ministry our father the bishop (metropolitan) Abba ___, and for our orthodox bishops

3. Pray for this Holy Church (Monastery) and our assemblies

4. 5. and 6. are each "Lord have mercy."

After this, the deacons prostrate themselves before the altar and exit the sanctuary with their left foot first and stand to the right, facing the North, while the Priest/Bishop continues censing. Once he is finished, the deacons may return to the sanctuary.

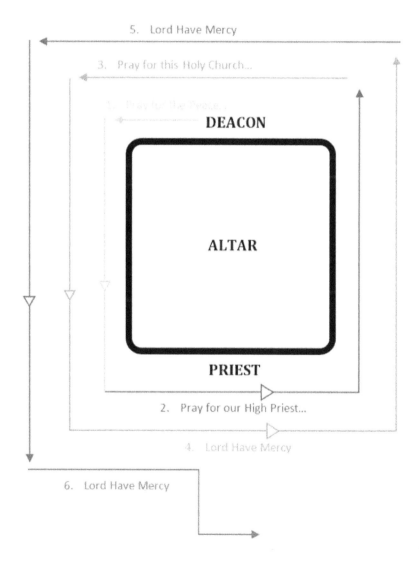

5. Lord Have Mercy

3. Pray for this Holy Church...

1. Pray for the Peace...

DEACON

ALTAR

PRIEST

2. Pray for our High Priest...

4. Lord Have Mercy

6. Lord Have Mercy

6. PRAYER OF RECONCILIATION

6. PRAYER OF RECONCILIATION

PRAYER OF RECONCILIATION AND THE LITURGY OF THE FAITHFUL

After the delivery of the weekly sermon, the congregation will recite the creed and the priest will commence the Prayer of Reconciliation.

The reconciliation prayer is beautiful and very moving. The first part of the prayer speaks of the reconciliation between heaven and earth – a 'vertical' reconciliation. The second part speaks of reconciliation between each other – a 'horizontal' reconciliation. See how in the very subject matter of this prayer, the sign of the cross is traced out , with the cross being the source of our reconciliation with God and where Jesus is our Mediator.

BUT WHY DO WE NEED A MEDIATOR?

The story of salvation is by far the greatest love story ever told. It would take multiple lifetimes to cover all the contemplations on the topic. It is so rich and deep.

In the beginning, God created everything seen and unseen...God created the heavens and the earth, the stars and the oceans, the mountains and the rivers, the birds and every other animal, yet above all, God created humanity, Adam and Eve, the pinnacle and crown of creation. God, Adam and Eve lived in great peace and unity with one another, with an incredible bond; taking walks in the beautiful garden of Eden, discovering and naming new animals and species of flowers.

They would swim in waterfalls, hike up mountains, climb the highest trees, play with lions and eat the sweetest fruits – life was perfect. Then one day humanity for a single moment turned its attention from God, sinned and fell and it was all downhill from there. We became separated from God and we needed someone to fill that gap. Despite humanity recognising its fault, it was too late, sin had entered the world; and with sin comes its consequence – death. This death and corruption grew in the heart of humanity and with each generation, humanity grew further and further separate from God. Humanity strayed from the path God intended. But God did not lose hope in the crown of His creation and used the most loving methods He could to bring humanity back on the right path. From tough love laws, like the like the 10 commandments, to great wonders like the 10 plagues to save his people from slavery in Egypt. From prophets with messages of intense passionate love, like Hosea, to prophets with messages of deep lamenting sadness, like Jeremiah. All to try and show His desire to reunite with humanity and to bring us back onto the right path. However, humanity just kept betraying and disobeying the One who loved them the most.

Yet no matter how much humanity rejected the Lord, despite all of humanity's disobedience and refusal to fix the bond with God; God still loved and refused to stop loving man. He was faithful even when we

What the Fathers Say

Our Lord Jesus Christ, the Word of God, of His boundless love, became what we are that He might make us what He himself is"

– St Irenaeus

What the Fathers Say

Since with all my soul I behold the face of my beloved, therefore all the beauty of his form is seen in me

– St Gregory of Nyssa

were faithless. He loved us even when we were unlovable. Truly we were, and still are, the most favoured of all of God's creation. Some humans tried to reconcile with God and the Lord provided an avenue for them to reconnect and somewhat patch this separation – introducing... the Old Testament priesthood. These priests would make daily sacrifices and yearly offerings to intercede and mediate between God and humanity with the aim of filling the gap of separation with blood sacrifices. The thing is, it didn't really cut it, it was like a "duct tape solution". It wasn't really fixing the problem it was just addressing some of the symptoms. The actual disease is sin and death. It would be like giving tissues to someone who is sneezing, sure you've addressed the symptom of sneezing but the underlying illness is the flu and tissues won't fix the flu.

I used to carpool with my old neighbour. He had this special 'water feature' in his car - whenever it rained and he broke hard enough, all the water that built up in his sunroof would pour out onto the person sitting in the passenger seat. It turns out his 'water feature' was simply a hole in his sunroof. So whenever it rained my neighbour and I would travel around and pick up our friends and go out for a drive. The unsuspecting victim would sit in the passenger seat, and at the right moment... bam! My neighbour would hit the brakes and all the rainwater would drench our friend, and naturally we would crack up laughing. Over time, everyone caught onto the joke so my neighbour got some duct tape and taped up the hole. One day, after a long rainy week, my neighbour's mum needed a lift. On the way, for whatever reason, my neighbour hit the brakes!...and all the water that built up over the weeks, broke through the duct tape, and soaked my neighbours mum...needless to say he fixed the hole properly after that.

The Old Testament priesthood was like that duct tape solution; it never fixed the problem, it just created a temporary patch. It wasn't even able to fully identify the problem and even if it did identify the main components of the problem, it couldn't fix it. Humanity needed a permanent fix, an ultimate sacrifice that would be the final sacrifice. We needed someone to mediate between God and humanity, permanently, a once and for all, to abolish the enmity and remove the bitterness between humanity and God. To break down that wall of sin and separation. Only Jesus Christ could be that mediator, that true high priest. Christ is the one who came and offered the final blood sacrifice, the only one that really mattered. He was the ultimate sacrifice that ended all sacrifices. So when Christ came and mediated between God and humanity, he bridged the separation, filling it with Himself through His Incarnation, life, death, resurrection and ascension. And, being fully human, His ascension into heaven made it possible for all of humanity to come up to heaven with Him, if only we unite with Him by

What the Fathers Say

A gift offered to God is not acceptable unless the giver puts aside his or her anger and becomes reconciled to their brother or sister

– Chromatius

What the Fathers Say

Sick, our nature demanded to be healed; fallen, to be raised up; dead, to rise again... Closed in the darkness, it was necessary to bring us the light; captives, we awaited a Savior... Are these things minor or insignificant? Did they not move God to descend to human nature and visit it, since humanity was in so miserable and unhappy a state?

— St Gregory of Nyssa

participating in and communing with His life, death and resurrection.

When He incarnated, He became one with us and united humanity with the divine.

When He lived He taught us how to live divine.

When He died, He sacrificed for us showing us how to love divine.

When He rose, He resurrected us and made us immortally divine.

And when He ascended He brought us up to heaven with Him in His kingdom divine.

As St Athanasius says, "He took what is ours and gave us what is His".

And now God and humanity are united once more.

"[He] became for us a mediator with the Father, and the middle wall You have broken down and the old enmity You have abolished. You have reconciled the earthly with the heavenly and made the two into one, and fulfilled the economy in the flesh." – The Liturgy of St Gregory.

This prayer of reconcilliation from the Liturgy of St Gregory is not only a reminder that we are now reconciled with God, but that to remain reconciled with God, we must always be reconciled with one another. The Prayer of Reconciliation is not just highlighting that God reconciled with us, but that we must follow His example. It is another reminder that if we wish to be in the presence of God, then we too must reconcile with all, even our enemies.

GREET ONE ANOTHER WITH A HOLY KISS

– 2 CORINTHIANS 13:12

The priest reaches a certain section of the Prayer of Reconciliation where the deacon calls out to the people and tells them to "greet one another with a holy kiss". At its core the "holy kiss" or the "kiss of peace" is just a greeting. It is a gesture symbolising that all who partake of it, are at peace with one another. In the early church, the regular method of greeting was with a kiss, as is still the same in many cultures. Thus the kiss of peace was literally a kiss. Today, in the Catholic church, during this section, the people simply shake hands, which has the exact same meaning, only with a different gesture. The greeting symbolises peace, unity and love between one another. Those exchanging the kiss of peace should be saying, "Christ is between us," and the other replying, "He is and always will be." Alternatively, they may say, "Peace be with you," the other replying with, "and also with you."

I am sure everyone has heard that you cannot partake of the mysteries while being upset at someone or whilst you have angered another. This is a direct teaching of the Lord.

"Therefore if you bring your gift to the altar, and there remember that your brother

One who does not love one's brother does not love the Lord.

– St Cyril of Alexandria

Let brotherly peace come first, before one approaches the altar

– St Jerome

has something against you, leave your gift there before the altar, and go your way. First be reconciled to your brother, and then come and offer your gift." – Matthew 5:23-24.

Many may think this isn't such a big deal; God is merciful and understands that we can't forgive someone because perhaps what they did was so terrible or because we are too ashamed. The Fathers of the church disagree very strongly with refusing to obey Christ's instruction here. Just read what some of the Fathers have said:

"Jesus does not even receive the sacrifice of worship without the sacrifice of love. Not before or later but precisely while the very gift is lying there, when the sacrifice is already beginning, he sends you to be reconciled to your brother." – St John Chrysostom.

We may find it hard to reconcile with certain people, especially our enemies, to the point that it may feel like a kind of suffering. What needs to be understood is that forgiving is not easy and being at peace with all is very hard. To go against our own will and forgive or ask for forgiveness is almost a small, personal crucifixion; it is obedience to the life of cruciformity. However, that is exactly what we need to do if we are to fully reconcile with God and man; we must live a life of crucifixion as Jesus did – the life of cruciformity!

When Jesus was on the cross He said, "Father, forgive them." So whatever excuse you may have doesn't really compare to the forgiveness Christ showed on the cross. Even if those angry at us do not accept our apology or seek our forgiveness, we must do our part; walk the path of the Via Dolorosa, to Golgotha and there crucify our wills and apologise and forgive.

THE APOCALYPSE

Apocalypse! Such a scary word. It's associated with pain, suffering, destruction and of course, the end of the world! However, the word apocalypse comes from the Greek word "apokalypsis" which literally means "unveiling".

So what's the point of this short word study? Well, at this point in the liturgy, the priest lifts up a triangular veil above his head. It is lifted in a way that it covers his eyes from seeing the "embrace of the Father". As this is happening, a deacon comes and stands between the veiled priest and the Embrace of the Father, and holds up a cross. The priest continues to try and gaze at the Embrace of the Father, but cannot see Him because the veil is in his way. This is the scene until the priest says the words, "in Christ Jesus our Lord"; at which point the priest removes the veil over his eyes and sees the cross held by the deacon and the image of the Jesus in the Embrace of the Father behind the deacon. He also removes the veil of the prospherine off the altar such that the Body and Blood are now visible.

> **What the Fathers Say**
>
> *Our life and our death is with our neighbor. If we gain our brother, we have gained God, but if we scandalize our brother, we have sinned against Christ*
>
> *– St Anthony the Great*

This whole scene is beyond beautiful. Let's break it down. The priest here is a symbol of humanity after the fall. Humanity was constantly trying to gaze upon God but couldn't because of the "veil" of separation and sin that we brought upon ourselves. We were blind. No matter what we did, we could never fully gaze upon God nor be in His full presence nor develop a completely perfect and intimate relationship with Him because we had the veil of sin and separation blocking us. Then, one amazing day, "Christ Jesus our Lord" came and stood before God and man on the cross and became the bridge overcoming the separation. Through the cross, Christ the Mediator between God and man removed the veil from the eyes of humanity and showed us the image of the Father in Himself, the image of perfect Love, on the cross, for the salvation

REFLECTION

The Prayer of Reconcilliation retells the story of our salvation. Hence, the prayer allows us to focus on reconcilliation with God after we fell. Having a focus for your prayer is an effective tool in achieving successful prayer.

of the whole world. So that whatever was veiled before may be unveiled. That there may be an apocalypse and a reconciliation. We can now say with the man born blind "I was blind, now I see" (John 9:25).

Not only is the veil over our eyes removed, but the veil that is covering the altar – the prospherine – is also removed. So that there is even an apocalypse, an unveiling of the Body and Blood of Christ on the altar, for all to see.

However, this unveiling goes even deeper. If the unveiled image of God Himself, and our now unveiled, unrestricted relationship with God isn't touching enough, then check this out. We always hear that God is our true Bridegroom, our one true love. There is only one major time that comes to mind where an unveiling happens – at a wedding, when the bride is unveiled for her groom. So that the two may stare at each other in love and in excitement for the future they will share together. So that they may say, "Yes this is my bride", "Yes this is my groom." This moment in the liturgy is also a bridal unveiling. By the cross, the bride of Christ, the church, is unveiled for Christ to see. Likewise, Christ the true Bridegroom is unveiled for the church to see. So they may say, "Yes this is the church, My bride. I am hers", "Yes this is Christ, my Bridegroom. I am His."

THE EMBRACE OF THE FATHER?

The Embrace of the Father is the curved section at the very east of the church. It is in the sanctuary directly in front of the altar. It has various other names, the most common of which is "apse". The apse has very interesting pharaonic roots and relates to a story of one of the ancient Egyptian goddesses and the structure of her temple. However, more relevant is its beautiful Christian meaning. The curved section, as the name suggests, literally symbolises God the Father hugging the church. In the centre of the embrace, there is a painting of Christ on His Throne with the heavenly hosts all around Him. This is how God the Father hugged the world, through the person of Christ, by sending Him and revealing Him to us. A hug is a symbol of love, thus the symbol of the Father's love for the world is in the embrace and union of Christ's divinity with his humanity in the incarnation. This love is reflected in the all-famous verse "For God so loved the world that He gave His only begotten Son, that whoever believes in Him should not perish but have everlasting life" (John 3:16).

A nice contemplation is that it's as though God gave us a big hug by sending Christ into the world and is still hugging us through the church that keeps us spiritually safe, just as a mother hugs her child. This is why, if you look from a top view, you may find that many churches have positioned their pews and chairs in a semi-circular pattern facing the altar, as if to hug the Father back, forming a full circle with the embrace of the Father.

We the church are acknowledging the warm tender hug of God and in turn are hugging Him back, while keeping the altar at the heart of our embrace. The altar, of course, being the place where Christ is, who is the centrepoint of the liturgical experience as the mediator between God and man, for He is fully God and fully Man.

NO ONE KNOWS THE THINGS OF GOD EXCEPT THE SPIRIT OF GOD

In the early church before reciting the creed, the catechumens and those who were not going to partake of the Eucharist would be asked to leave the church as the liturgy of the faithful was about to begin. Only those who were to have communion were allowed to stay, meaning even those who received the Holy Spirit and were members of the church that were not having holy communion for any reason were supposed to leave.

Today, before the recital of the creed, the deacon says, "In the wisdom of God let us attend..." but years ago there was an additional part that has since been removed, "The doors, the doors. In the wisdom of God let us attend..." This was a signal from the deacons to the subdeacon to ensure that all non-believers had left the church and that all the doors were locked, as the reciting of the creed was about to take place and was strictly for the faithful only. It may seem a little

---

What the Fathers Say

These things we also speak, not in words which man's wisdom teaches but which the Holy Spirit teaches, comparing spiritual things with spiritual. But the natural man does not receive the things of the Spirit of God, for they are foolishness to him; nor can he know them, because they are spiritually discerned"

– 1 Corinthians 2:11-15

exclusive but it was actually an act of mercy. It is impossible for anyone to truly understand and believe the creed or the rest of the Liturgy of the Faithful without the grace of the Holy Spirit, a gift that catechumens had not yet received. If any should hear these things without the gift of the Holy Spirit, it would be very confusing and may cause more harm than good.

OFFER, OFFER, OFFER IN ORDER

If you ever notice the deacon's proclamation to "greet one another with the holy kiss" we get to a bit of text which seems out of place, "Offer. Offer. Offer in order..." The reason for this is that in the early church the deacon would proclaim that all should greet one another with a kiss of peace, and once the kiss was offered all the catechumens would be departing at that time and the deacon would stop proclaiming until all catechumens had left. Then the deacon would

People, Places &Things

Godparents in the early church

At this stage of the liturgy, there was an important role for godparents to play. Godparents were those Christians who would take care of people they or the church thought were suitable candidates for baptism (catechumens). They would teach them the *faith and disciple them spiritually. The godparent would stand next to the catechumen and explain all the happenings and readings of the Liturgy of the Word/ Catechumens. During the kiss of peace, the godparents and the catechumens would say their goodbyes, as the catechumens left the church.*

continue "yes, Lord, who is Jesus Christ the Son of God, hear us and have mercy upon us." Once the doors of the church had been shut, the deacon would continue his proclamation to the faithful saying, "Offer. Offer. Offer in order..." and the faithful would bring forth their gifts. In fact, in various liturgy books we find this response divided, being punctuated with the heading "Anaphora" just before the section of "Offer. Offer. Offer in order..."

The Agape meal is a free meal that is held directly after the liturgy. If you have ever been to an Orthodox liturgy, especially in the lands of immigration where parish sizes are smaller, you would notice that after the liturgy everyone is usually eating. I am sure many think it's a cultural practice (just go to a Mediterranean household and you will understand). The truth is, if you were to retrace the origins of this meal, you would find its roots derive from the Agape meal of the early church. It was a meal hosted by the church where all the members would bring an offering of money, bread, wine, fruits, candles, oil, firewood, vegetables, and sometimes even fully prepared dishes. These were presented during the liturgy on the prospherine when the deacon would proclaim, "Offer, Offer, Offer..." From the same offering, what was necessary for the liturgical services was taken and the rest was split up for the agape gathering.

From the same cloth came the meal of the Eucharist and the meal of agape.

Everyone gave something. It was a physical representation that you are a part, an active participant in the

Body of Christ. Even if you had nothing to give, there was a well or body of water often on the church grounds; those who had nothing would go fill up a jug of water from this well and offer it to the Lord.

This was so pivotal that the monks in the early centuries used to build the dining room directly attached to the church, so that once the liturgy was finished and the monks had all shared the True Meal for the spirit – the Body and Blood of Christ – they would without delay share a second meal for the body, in unity and fellowship. This Agape meal was thus an extension of the Eucharist, highlighting the incredible importance God places on unity, fellowship and love. Remember Agape means "Love", specifically divine Love, the self-emptying Love of God made manifest in Christ's incarnation, life and death. The Agape meal put all people on equal ground so that even the poor and the rich were all eating together on the same table, being members of the same Body of Christ who have made Him their common ground. Just as Christ emptied Himself, so too did rich and poor empty themselves of any social status they may have held outside the church.

7. LITURGY OF THE FAITHFUL

7. LITURGY OF THE FAITHFUL

The Liturgy of the Faithful technically starts once the prospherine (altar covering) is removed. The prospherine symbolises the stone that sealed Christ's tomb, and so – when the offerings on the altar are covered with the prospherine after the prayer of thanksgiving – this represents Christ's burial. On the other hand, the removal of the prospherine which heralds the beginning of the Liturgy of the Faithful represents the removal of the stone from the door of the tomb; it is a symbol of the resurrection of Jesus. The fluttering movement of the prospherine with the noise of the bells that are sewn to it reminds us of the angels that were fluttering around the tomb and the earthquake that accompanied the resurrection.

Coming as it does after the Prayer of Reconcilliation, the removal of the prospherine highlights that reconciliation between God and man, between heaven and earth, has been completed through the resurrection of Jesus from the dead.

For those who are paying close attention at this point of the liturgy, the priest is moving the altar cloths in a specific sequence that has some interesting symbolism.

Before the priest says "The Lord be with you all" and blesses the congregation, he takes the cloth that was once on top of the prospherine and places it on his left hand, but with his right hand he holds the cloth that used to cover the body of Christ in the paten. With this cloth that covered the body, the priest blesses the church and in doing so he pleads with the congregation to "lift up your hearts" to the Lord. It is as if the priest is showing that the cloth which once symbolised death – that was used to cover a dead body – now symbolises life! Just as the disciples who visited the empty tomb saw the linen cloths and believed, likewise the priest is showing the linen cloth, the evidence of the resurrection, to the whole congregation so that they may see and believe, lifting up their hearts to the resurrected God.

LIFT UP YOUR HEARTS

How can we lift up our hearts?

It is hard to lift up your heart when it is being weighed down with the cares of this world. Your heart is like a balloon that wants to ascend to heaven but tying this balloon down are the cares of the world: my Instagram followers, what I am wearing, what others are wearing, problems with my parents or friends, my personal anxieties. All these things weigh down your heart and stop it from floating to

Marriage Supper

One of the symbols of the liturgy is that of a marriage supper or wedding feast (Revelation 19:9). The lifting of the prospherine and unveiling of the altar therefore represents *Christ the groom lifting the veil of the bride so that they are no longer separated but united as one Body with Christ as the Head.*

People, Places &Things

heaven. To lift up your heart you first need to cut off these strings that tie you down.

A very useful practice in this case is to make whatever distraction that is tying you down the subject of your prayer. So when you are faced with thoughts of problems at home or school, spend sometime during the liturgy pray about this issue. If my anxiety is distancing me from the people around me and I am missing out on their fellowship, then I should ask the Lord to teach me to be anxious for nothing. This way you have transformed your problem from a distraction to a means of connection with God.

HOLY, HOLY, HOLY

The priest prays "Agios" (Holy) three times, with a very long and moving tune. This tune is designed to help us focus our hearts and minds on the mystery and majesty of God. At the chanting of the first "Holy" the priest makes the sign of the cross on himself, at the second "Holy" he signs the altar servants and lastly he signs the congregation. In many places in the Bible, the congregation of the Lord are called "the saints", for God has sanctified us all. What is amazing is that, while the priest speaks to God and calls Him Holy, he gestures towards us human beings also calling us holy! God is Holy by nature, whereas we His people partake in His holiness by grace.

The priest prays "Agios" (Holy) three times, with a very long and moving tune. This tune is designed to help us focus our hearts and minds on the mystery and majesty of God. At the chanting of the first "Holy" the priest makes the sign of the cross on himself, at the second "Holy" he signs the altar servants and lastly he signs the congregation. In many places in the Bible, the congregation of the Lord are called "the saints", for God has sanctified us all. What is amazing is that, while the priest speaks to God and calls Him Holy, he gestures towards us human beings also calling us holy! God is Holy by nature, whereas we His people partake in His holiness by grace.

Fr Mark Basily shared with me this experience during his mission trip to Kenya: "When I was in Kenya I prayed a Liturgy with an African priest who was praying in the Swahili language. The words made no sense to me but I noticed one word that kept being repeated. That word was Takatifo! Nearly every few lines that word kept being repeated. I became curious what this word meant so at the end of the Liturgy I asked the priest what does Takatifo mean? He replied 'it means "holy"'. I never realised how many times we repeat the word 'holy'! The Liturgy is all about placing ourselves in God's holy presence and sharing with the angels in their praise of His holiness – and in turn He makes us holy".

What the Fathers Say

"Since we are the portion of the Holy One, let us do all those things which pertain to holiness"

– St. Clement of Rome

This is a nice reminder that we should aim to see the holiness of God in one another, because the incarnation of Christ has sanctified human nature and made each of us holy. The signing of the cross together with the chanting of, "holy" is an affirmation, a declaration, that God has made us holy as God is Himself Holy: "... that we should be holy and without blame before Him in love" (Ephesians 1:4) and "...as He who called you is holy, you also be holy in all your conduct, because it is written, 'Be holy, for I am holy'" (1 Peter 1:15,16).

The late Fr Feltaous the Syrian tells a story that happened to him when he heard the news of the passing of HH Pope Kyrillos VI. Pope Kyrillos and Fr Feltaous were very close and HH had made a promise to Fr Feltaous that he would always be there for him. When HH passed away Fr Feltaous was very upset, and while crying he looked at a picture of Pope Kyrillos VI and shouted, "How could you leave me!? You promised you would never leave me! How could you break your promise!?" All of a sudden, Pope Kyrillos

Holinesss

The primary Old Testament word for holiness in Hebrew means 'to cut or to separate' Fundamentally, holiness is a cutting off or separation from what is unclean, and a consecration to what is pure. In the New Testament, the word for holy in Greek, Agios, is the same root word for saint and sanctified. Similarly, in Coptic the word used in the liturgy for "holy" is "ekoab", which also means "saint". So the priest, in crossing all and saying holy, is in fact calling us saints.

appeared and a dialogue broke out between them. HH explained to Fr Feltaous that he would still never leave him and there was no difference between his help on earth and his help from heaven. After finally calming Fr Feltaous down Pope Kyrillos says these departing words, "Do you want to know the difference between heaven and earth? Those on earth look up and see the saints in heaven and those in heaven look down and see the saints on earth..."

This story is so fascinating! Even heaven recognises us on earth as saints! Not because of any goodness in us but because God made us this way, in His image and likeness. It is up to us to keep this image of God in us. We know how the saints in heaven did it so it is smart to walk in the same path the saints did. To live the life the saints lived. The life of prayer and service, the life of voluntary submission and willing obedience to God.

Up until a few years ago (and in some of our sister churches to this day), two deacons stood at the Royal Door of the sanctuary, one on each side, when the hymn of the cherubim was sung, "The cherubim worship you... proclaiming and saying, "Holy, Holy, Holy..." Each deacon held a rod with a fan made of peacock feathers attached to the end. The deacons would wave these fans up and down, reminding us of the wings of the cherubim and seraphim in heaven. Often these poles and feathers would have small bells attached to them to imitate the sound of the fluttering wings of the angels in heaven.

This practice reminds us of the great honour God has granted us by allowing us to "share in the hymn of the cherubim" (Liturgy of St Gregory).

"YOU HAVE NOT ABANDONED US"

One of the most moving prayers in the liturgy is said here, "you have not abandoned us." It is said with a moving tune and really pulls at the heartstrings of the focused listener. If you are going through a difficult time, these words provide great comfort to you. It doesn't say that all problems go away, or that life will get easy, it says that in all our hardships and afflictions, God is there with

REFLECTION

When we reach this section pray with all your heart: "Lord, help me see that you do not abandon me in this task, journey or trial. I ask that you hold me when I go through it, for I can do all things through You. I pray that I never abandon You as You will never abandon me.

us. Further, Isaiah says of God's children, "In all their distress, to Him there was distress" (Isaiah 63:9), which means that whatever distress we go through, God goes through the same distress with us.

In Kenya, the church set up a service called Raha house. This is a house for young boys who had been abandoned by their families and had taken refuge in the streets. The servants go around and collect all of these boys that are willing to come, giving them a home, food and schooling. I recall spending time with a young child named Dwate. Dwate's mother was a severe drug addict who had abandoned him on the streets when he was only 3 years old. He was left completely traumatised and does not speak except to very few people.

After a few months, Dwate really warmed up to me and began to spend a lot of time with me and to speak to me – he trusted me. One day Dwate was very sick and he needed a needle but he was too scared. The thing is, if he didn't get the needle he would die. So as he was rolling around in pain, refusing to get treatment, he was calling out "Meena, Meena". So the servants called me from my compound to the Raha house to help Dwate. When I arrived he kept saying "nina hofu, je ituamiza", "I am scared, is it going to hurt?" I said "ndiyo, lakini nitakukumbatia", "yes, but I will hold you the whole time!" I felt so much pain for him, I felt his fear, I felt him shaking in my arms. That's how God feels when we go through pain. He wants to free us more than

What the Fathers Say

"God whispers to us in our pleasures, speaks in our conscience, but shouts in our pains."

– C.S. Lewis

we ourselves want to be freed, but to be truly free, we need the needle! We need the pain in our lives so God can take us where we need to go, so we can be healed just as Dwate was.

There are so many positives that come out of pain and distress. They are the travel companions the Lord uses to take us down the path of perfection. God doesn't remove our distress, but he will never abandon us. He holds us tightly in His arms when we go through our tribulations. With God we can take on anything but without Him we cannot conquer even the smallest task. So "rejoice when you fall into various trials and tribulations", knowing that this is the time that God is the closest to you. You may not hear Him, you may not see Him, you may not feel his presence at all, but he is closer to you than you realise, He is in your very heart. He will never abandon you!

The SPOON FROM HEAVEN

There are so many beautiful words in this prayer but a favourite of many is when the priest chants, "Was incarnate and became Man..." This speaks about the moment when the glory of God meets the frailty of humanity – Christ becomes Man bringing Heaven to earth so that earth may be raised up to Heaven. This is symbolised by the priest placing a spoonful of incense in the censer (as we said earlier, the censer resembles the womb of St Mary).

What will be the result? Will the evil in men's hearts destroy the goodness in Christ, or will His goodness triumph? At the end of this part we hear, "He descended into Hades through the Cross". It seems He has lost...

There is an old rubric that has been revived in recent years. It involves the spoon; the priest uses the same spoon that is used for distributing the Blood, to place incense in the censer at the words, "Was incarnate and became man..."

The communion spoon is kept on top of the throne when the priest sets up the altar and it remains there throughout the liturgy until communion. However, at this point in the liturgy, the priest reaches under the cloth that covers the throne and moves the spoon down. He then uses it to put a spoonful of incense into the censer (held up by the deacon), carefully wiping it clean of any residue of incense, and then returns it again on top of the throne. Embodied in this little rubric is a rich metaphor of our salvation. Let's break it down:

• The spoon on top of the throne represents Christ before the incarnation, sitting upon His throne in heavenly glory.

• Removing the spoon from the throne is the descent of the Word of God from heavenly glory to earthly humility (Philippians 2:5-8).

• He came to earth, even to the womb of the Virgin (represented by the censer).

What the Fathers Say

"The Teacher of children became himself a child among children, that he might instruct the unwise. The Bread of heaven came down to earth to feed the hungry."

–St. Cyril of Jerusalem

"Christ in the flesh, rejoice with trembling and with joy; with trembling because your sins are forgiven, with joy because of your hope."

– St. Gregory Nazianzen

• He immersed His divinity (the spoon) in our humanity (the incense) and emerged united with us as fully human while being fully divine (the spoon is now filled with incense).

• Having become Man, He offered Himself as a sweet smelling sacrifice for our salvation on the Cross (the incense burning in the censer is itself destroyed but in dying, it gives a sweet aroma to all who smell it).

• With this sacrifice, He wiped away our sins (the priest wiping the residue of incense from the spoon).

• But after His death, He was hidden from us for three days (the spoon being hidden in the cloth as the priest wipes it).

• Then He rose from the dead (the spoon emerges from within the cloth) and ascended back into heaven (the spoon being placed back on top of the throne where it was originally).

• In heaven, Christ is once again invisible to us (covered by the cloth on top of the throne), but we know He will come back to us to judge the world and take those who loved Him into the wedding feast, an eternal joy of unity with Him, in His kingdom (the unveiling of the throne at the end of the liturgy in order to remove the cup and to administer Holy Communion to the faithful).

The next section that clearly stands out is, "He rose from the dead..." This is the ultimate triumph of God's glory over the frailty of humanity. Of course He couldn't lose! Through His Resurrection, He broke the power of Hades over us. In the traditional Coptic tune, the words "He rose" are prayed with a loud and triumphant melody, like a thousand trumpets blaring out the news to the whole world!

St Athanasius wrote that the coming of Christ into the world was like the sun shining on a pile of rotting rubbish. The powerful sunlight can bleach and sterilise the rubbish, but the rubbish can never taint the sunlight. Thus also, all the shame and evil of humanity could never overcome the holy glory of God in Christ – not even death could conquer Him.

8. INSTITUTION NARRATIVE

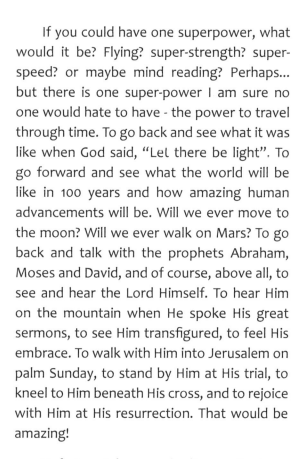

8. INSTITUTION NARRATIVE

FROZEN IN TIME...

If you could have one superpower, what would it be? Flying? super-strength? super-speed? or maybe mind reading? Perhaps... but there is one super-power I am sure no one would hate to have - the power to travel through time. To go back and see what it was like when God said, "Let there be light". To go forward and see what the world will be like in 100 years and how amazing human advancements will be. Will we ever move to the moon? Will we ever walk on Mars? To go back and talk with the prophets Abraham, Moses and David, and of course, above all, to see and hear the Lord Himself. To hear Him on the mountain when He spoke His great sermons, to see Him transfigured, to feel His embrace. To walk with Him into Jerusalem on palm Sunday, to stand by Him at His trial, to kneel to Him beneath His cross, and to rejoice with Him at His resurrection. That would be amazing!

Unfortunately, we don't exactly have this greatly desired super-power. We do, however, have access to something that's pretty close... a time machine - the time machine of the liturgy. Every liturgy we travel thousands of years back in time and relive the moment Christ offered Himself for us on the Cross. The church takes us back and allows us to partake of this exact event with

Christ through the prayer of the "Institution Narrative", also known as the anamnesis - the Greek word for "remember". The anamnesis is a point where past and future all converge into a single moment – the present. At the Last Supper, Christ took his disciples forward in time to His crucifixion, offering them His Body and Blood the day before He broke it and shed it on the Cross. In like manner, the church today takes us back in time to the Cross, where on the altar Christ is offering us the very same Body and Blood that he broke and shed on the Cross for our salvation.

For roughly the first 100 years of the history of the church, this section was the only formal part of the liturgy. The rest of the prayers were added later and formalised based on the practices of each culture at the time. History shows that the "Institution Narrative" has origins that precede the four gospel accounts. In fact, the first liturgy ever formally written is said to have been penned by the great St Mark, the author of the second gospel account and the founder of the church in Egypt.

What the Fathers Say

"If the poison of pride is swelling up in you, turn to the Eucharist; and that Bread, Which is your God humbling and disguising Himself, will teach you humility."

– St Cyril of Alexandria

HE BROKE IT

There is one line in the anamnesis that tends to give everyone goosebumps. The priest says, "He broke it and gave it to His own holy disciples and saintly apostles saying, "Take, eat of it all of you, for this is My Body…""

The most vivid image in the entire liturgy has to be right here. Although Christ broke His Body for us at the last supper, He literally broke His Body for us on the cross – breaking the flesh of His Body and shedding His Blood. If you notice, many priests, whilst breaking the Bread at this point, exaggerate the break. "He broke it" – every time it is said, it feels as though our time machine has taken us right to the moment Christ offered Himself on the Cross, and by extension Christ offering Himself to his disciples at the Last Supper. In all three cases, it is the exact same Body and Blood – whether at the Cross, or at the Last Supper, or as the priest stands at the altar in the Divine Liturgy. Every Holy Communion

What the Fathers Say

If the fever of selfish greed rages in you, feed on this Bread; and you will learn generosity. If the cold wind of coveting withers you, hasten to the Bread of Angels; and charity will come to blossom in your heart.

– St. Cyril of Alexandria

REFLECTION

Am I always the first to speak, or do I take a moment to listen first?

throughout all of time is a re-living of Christ's once and for all sacrifice on the Cross. I have a scene in my mind. When Christ first broke this Holy Communion with His disciples and said, "Take eat of it all of you", He was not only looking at His disciples, but also beyond them, as though there were others in the upper room with them, as though we, and all of the church throughout all of time, were in there with them, with Him.

Christ's blood was shed...as a sacrifice...

A sacrifice implies giving up something of less value for something of relatively greater value. We sacrifice social activities (less value) so we can study and achieve our best marks (greater value). We sacrifice yummy foods so we can lose weight and become healthy... but what is greater than God? How can God ever be of less value than anything? Where is the greater good in God sacrificing Himself for us? What sacrifice would be worth the death of Christ? How could He sacrifice Himself for us?

This sacrifice cannot be measured by our own human scales! In the Old Testament, it was the life of an animal that was sacrificed on behalf of a human... but the life of God on behalf of a human doesn't seem to be a fair trade. St Augustine says "He died for all of us as if there were only one of us... and even if you were the only person on earth, Christ would have still come and died for you" How? How could our lives – with all our pettiness and sinfulness – be worth more than God's?

> ### What the Fathers Say
>
> *If you feel the itch of intemperance, nourish yourself with the Flesh and Blood of Christ, Who practiced heroic self-control during His earthly life; and you will become temperate.*
>
> *– St. Cyril of Alexandria*

How could He see us as worthy of dying for?

But God does not work by our system. He does not work by the measure of human logic but by the measure of Divine love! "Love and pain go together" how true this is in the case of Christ... in this pain and sacrifice we see love!

Christ didn't look to those crucifying Him and smite them, He didn't see hypocritical proud Jews as deserving of cursing, he didn't see oppressive Roman soldiers as deserving of hatred, he didn't see the right hand thief as deserving of Hades. Rather, through the sacrificial eyes of love, He saw His beloved children needing Him to be their healer, their mediator, their father, their friend, their guide and their sacrifice... to be our sacrifice... dying our death so we may rise in His resurrection...

AMEN, AMEN, AMEN

Finally, the priest pointing to the bread says "For every time you eat of this bread" then pointing to the wine, "and drink of this cup, you proclaim My death, confess My resurrection, and remember Me till I come."

Throughout the liturgy the people will confess their belief and affirmation in what is taking place on the altar, and also in how it actually took place in history by chanting, "Amen", or "I believe", or "We confess", but no hymn of belief is as affirming in the liturgy as the hymn, "Amen, Amen, Amen, Your death O Lord, we proclaim..." This hymn

What the Fathers Say

If you are lazy and sluggish about spiritual things, strengthen yourself with this heavenly Food; and you will grow fervent.

– St Cyril of Alexandria

seems to liven up the whole congregation. It is beautiful when sung together as a church and is very powerful. If there was any doubt about how you felt toward the Mystery in front of you, there usually is no doubt after this hymn. Throughout the Institution Narrative we pray "Amen" but here we affirm "Amen Amen Amen" to show our belief is of the highest level. This hymn proclaims our belief in the death, resurrection and ascension of Jesus. It acts as a mini creed and is positioned perfectly after the church relives the events that took place on the night of the Last Supper, and in turn Christ's offering on the cross.

It would have seemed as if all of time itself has stopped. We may not have any time-travel super-powers, but the church clearly does, to go back to the past, and to the future – to a foretaste of the kingdom of Heaven!

Many Liturgies

In the early church, the Institution was the only formal part of the liturgy. It was first written by St Mark. Today we have many liturgies in circulation within all the orthodox and apostolic churches, all of which are accepted as authentic.

However, today the Coptic Orthodox church only uses three of these liturgies. These are liturgies of St Basil, St Gregory and St Cyril.

People, Places &Things

LITURGY AND AMEN

What the Fathers Say

Lastly, if you feel scorched by the fever of impurity, go to the banquet of the Angels; and the spotless Flesh of Christ will make you pure and chaste.

– St Cyril of Alexandria

Sometimes, the liturgy can feel like a performance. With so much going on around you, a total sensory experience, it can be easy to just sit back and enjoy the show. It can be easy to think that the priests and deacons perform the liturgy and the rest are just a part of the audience. With this way of thinking, it is no wonder people feel no connection to the liturgy, the show must go on with or without us. However, if we understand the liturgy the way it is meant to be understood, we would know that without the people, there is no liturgy at all.

Liturgy or "Leitorgia" in Greek, comes from two root words. "Leitos", which means public, and "Ergos" which means work. So Liturgy is literally a "public work". Work implies effort, and not the effort of one or two people, but of the public, the entire congregation. Effort must be put in by the entire congregation, all must participate in the liturgy for it to actually be a liturgy at all.

We may not realise it, but without the people, there is no liturgy. The church highlights this for us in one powerful yet often overlooked word... "Amen." The word Amen is Hebrew for "Let it be". Without the "Amen" of the people, the prayers of the priests and deacons are incomplete. It is as though the people give their consent to the prayers and rituals, and without their "Amen" the prayers are not approved. When the people say "Amen" they are saying, "We agree and approve. We also believe, worship and partake."

Fr Thomas Hopko puts it this way, "If there's nobody there to say "Amen" to the bishop or priest's prayer, or they refuse to say "Amen", then the Liturgy stops. It's over. You can't go on. It has to be the "Amen" of all the gathering people who are faithful."

What the Fathers Say

"When, expecting someone whom we love, we put a beautiful tablecloth on the table and decorate it with candles and flowers, we do all this not out of necessity, but out of love. And the church is love, expectation and joy."
— Fr Alexander Schmemann.

REFLECTION

God's mercies are new every morning. Do I ask Him every day to have compassion on me and forgive me for my sins?

ANAMNESIS

"He broke it and said, 'Take, eat; this is My body which is broken for you; do this in remembrance of Me.'" 1 Corinthians 11:24

The word St. Paul used for "remembrance" in this verse is anamnesis, which is a Greek word which can be broken down into the word "amnesia", meaning "loss of memory", with the prefix "an-" meaning "not." Therefore, we are not just "remembering" the Last Supper but "not forgetting" it, which is not exactly the same thing. When we participate in the Eucharist, it is not simply a symbol or even a miraculous change in substance but rather our being present at the foot of the cross. The anamnesis is not just a call to remember, but a call to participate! To live in that moment of Christ's conquering of death and to continually relive that event every liturgy.

In the liturgy, anamnesis refers to a point where past and future all converge into a single moment. The Divine Liturgy is this single moment, where we relive and share in ("commemorate") Christ's "holy Passion, His Resurrection from the dead, His Ascension into the heavens, His Sitting at Your right hand, O Father, and His Second Coming from the heavens, awesome and full of glory".

9. Litanies and Commoration of saints

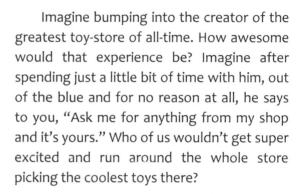

THE LITANIES

Imagine bumping into the creator of the greatest toy-store of all-time. How awesome would that experience be? Imagine after spending just a little bit of time with him, out of the blue and for no reason at all, he says to you, "Ask me for anything from my shop and it's yours." Who of us wouldn't get super excited and run around the whole store picking the coolest toys there?

Now imagine, instead of the creator of the coolest toy-store, it was the Creator of the universe. Imagine, out of His goodness and grace alone, He says to you, "Ask and you will receive" (John 16:24). What would you ask for? The Church right now has the Creator of the universe before us on the altar. We have been granted permission to ask whatever we desire. So the Church travels God's universe, choosing what it desires to ask for. So what does the Church ask for? The requests of the Church are written down in the section known as, the litanies.

The litanies are prayed in the following order:

1. The peace of the Church
2. The fathers the bishops
3. The presbyters and deacons
4. The places
5. Nature
6. The offerings
7. The commemoration of the saints and the prayer for the departed.

We all have things we want and need in life. Things like successful relationships, happy lives, successful careers and finances. But what is at the root of all these things we ask for? When we pray for successful relationships are we actually asking God to take away our fear of loneliness? When we we pray for successful careers are we actually praying for prestige and honour? Yet God is the greatest relationship we can seek, and all relationships will be successful when they stem from Him. God is the source of true joy and happiness for "In His presence is the fullness of joy" (Psalm 16). God is the One who gives us honour beyond this world and God is the only one on whom we should rely on for security. At the core of every personal prayer you will find either a virtue or a vice. But at the core of all the litanies you will find great virtue and pure intentions all for the glory of God and His people.

What the Fathers Say

He has instituted on His altar the sacrament of our peace and unity.

– St. Augustine

LITANY OF PEACE

When we pray for the peace of the Church, we are asking God to be in our midst always, that nothing shakes us and we always stay united with Him. The church is the house built upon the rock that no wave of the sea may destroy, yet throughout history the church has been in turmoil. Turmoils of persecution, martyrdom, heresy and division. Here we ask God to keep the church firm on the rock of the faith and for peace among all His children.

LITANY FOR THE POPE AND BISHOPS

When we pray for our fathers the bishops, we are asking God to guide our leaders and to equip them with all the tools needed to shepherd the flock of God to Him. They are the ones instructed with "dividing the word of truth" from those things which are not correct. They are to discern between what is heresy and what is correct teaching.

LITANY FOR THE PRIESTS

Our priests are the ones who are our direct guides throughout our journey to the kingdom of heaven. Here we ask God to also equip them with the tools needed to present us as acceptable offerings to the Lord. Just as the bishops, they too need much prayer that they may have the wisdom to lead with the humility to listen, and the love to serve with the faith to trust in God. The words that lead to life with the actions to back it up. We must never forget how much prayer our leaders need. They give up their lives for their love of

What the Fathers Say

You must follow the lead of the bishop, as Jesus Christ followed the lead of the Father; follow the presbytery as you would the Apostles; reverence the deacons as you would God's commandment.

– Ignatius of Antioch

People, Places &Things

"Papa"

The word pope is derived from the word "Papa" or "Baba" which more accurately translates to dad. This is what people called the bishop of Alexandria and was later taken and used also for the bishop of Rome. In reality the pope is just like every other bishop, however he is bishop over the principal diocese or see, the mother diocese and thus the bishop of the principal diocese is given a more respectful title of dad or pope.

God and His children so they must be granted the respect that comes with it.

LITANY FOR THE PLACES

The litany for the places is a prayer that God blesses the physical place and every place where His children preside. There is a story in the desert fathers where the demons appeared to St Macarius the Great and told him to leave the desert as it is the land of the demons. They explained to him that with his presence many holy men will follow and the land will no longer belong to the demons but will be a land belonging to God.

What the Fathers Say

The reason why I say that the presbyter prays for a city, village or for the whole world is that he must ask the Lord to forgive all those who pray.

– St. John Chrysostom

"Episkopos"

The title of bishop or "episkopos" comes from two ancient Greek root words: "epi-" meaning "over" and "skopos" meaning "to see or look". So the episkopos was one who would "over-see", one who is entrusted with the overall responsibility for the running of the church.

This sounds just like the pope and bishops today, they are to lead the servants, serving them in any way possible that allows the prosperity of their service while taking care of the Church, the house of God.

"Thirst for Jesus, that He may intoxicate you with His love. Close your eyes to the precious things of the world that you may deserve to have the peace of God reign in your heart. Abstain from the attractions which glitter before the eyes, that you may be worthy of joy in the Spirit."

– St Isaac the Syrian

LITANY FOR NATURE

When we pray for nature, we are asking that God bless our environment so that He may provide our livelihood for us. Remember that at the time the liturgy was written, most people would have been dependant on the crops of the land to survive, thus they needed good rain and successful harvests to obtain a livelihood. This litany is just as important for us today becasue the food that we eat today does not come from the supermarket as some may think but is grown in farms.

However, we do not pray for these things as one who sticks prayers into a vending machine hoping to get something we want out. Rather, we make our requests known to God our Father and ask that He, our true source of life, may provide our livelihood according to His will and what He knows to be best for us. We should have no fear that God will fail to provide because the bible is very clear that if He provides for the birds, how much more will He provide for us, He who gives "exceedingly abundantly above all we ask or know" (Ephesians 3:20).

One of the most precious lines in the whole liturgy is found here, "manage our lives as deemed fit". It is such a great request that can be so easily missed. It is a plea for God to intervene and do what is best for us. It is also a submission to God's will; by asking Him to manage, we are stepping aside and entrusting everything to Him. Note that here we are not asking for anything except that God do what He sees fit. St Isaac the Syrian says, "Do not ask God for anything that even without our request He takes care to give us. He does not hold these things from His housemates..." We are the ones living in the house of God from whom He does not withhold anything. He provides for us in every way and thus we ask Him to keep blessing and managing our lives as He has done so far.

"...for the eyes of everyone wait upon You, for You give them their food in due season. Deal with us according to Your goodness. O You who gives food to all flesh, fill our hearts with joy and gladness, that we too, having sufficiency in everything always may abound in every good deed."

The miracle of the feeding of the five thousand gives us an interesting insight into the sentiment of this prayer. Many of those who were fed miraculously by Christ followed Him only because their bellies had been filled. Christ rebuked them for this as their minds were focused on earthly needs rather than spiritual matters.

In this prayer we acknowledge that God is the source of our daily food. Even those who don't acknowledge their debt to God still receive their daily needs from His hand, whether they know it or not, for "He makes His sun to shine upon the righteous and the wicked" (Matthew 5:45). God loves everyone with infinite love and desires the salvation and perfection of everyone. We do acknowledge that He feeds us daily through nature, but we also go beyond that to ask for the gifts that really matter.

Our concern is for the heavenly bread that both fills and changes us. We do not just ask for the satisfaction of physical needs (which God grants to all without them even asking) but also for spiritual gifts, such as the gifts of joy and peace and love.

LITANY FOR THE OFFERINGS

Thus building on this, we have the litany of the offerings. Although the gifts on the altar were presented by people, the gifts themselves actually came from God. We would not have these gifts of bread and wine unless God had provided the rain, rich soil, fruitful trees, and so on. Thus the gifts we offer are actually from God Himself. It is like when we were young and wanted to buy our parents a Christmas present. We would take money from our parents and buy them a gift; although the gift came from our hands, it was really a gift that came from themselves. The beautiful thing is, our parents were so grateful and appreciative of the gift. Likewise God is overjoyed when we offer Him any offering, even though He is the true source of all good gifts.

DO NOT FORGET TO PRAY

Ultimately the best way to interact with the liturgy and to benefit from the litanies is when the priest and deacon ask you to pray for something... actually pray for it! The person this wish-list is sent to is not Santa, or your parents or anyone else, but rather God Himself and He said "ask and you shall receive" (Matthew 7:7). Ask for these good things from God with a pure heart and clean intentions and God will answer and give you, "... exceedingly abundantly above all that we ask or think" (Ephesians 3:20).

Actually pray for the pope and bishops, they have the hardest job in the world, to care for the entire church. They spend their entire day and stay up every night providing for the Church and those of their children in need and they never receive anything back for it.

Pray for rain because there are many farmers who lose all their lifestock in times of drought. Pray for the church to have peace and for the spread of the word of God to all the world. Everytime the deacon instructs the congregation to pray for something, pray!

COMMEMORATION OF THE SAINTS

What the Fathers Say

The daily invocation of the saints signify that God's saints live, and are near us and ever ready to help us. We live together with them in the house of our Heavenly Father only in different parts of it. We live in the earthly, they in the heavenly half; but we can converse with them, and they with us.

— St. John of Kronstandt.

Have you ever asked for something from dad and when he said no you went and asked your mum after? Then once she says yes you convince her to go and convince dad to agree to what you want as well? Of course you have. Basically, we do this because we know dad really struggles to say no to mum. Not that mum is more powerful or that dad is scared of mum (not in every household anyway) but because dad loves and respects mum and over time she has proved her genuineness and loyalty toward him. Thus, it is not that dad cannot say no to mum, but rather he doesn't want to... this is a power that needs to be exercised with great care, as the famous Spiderman quote says, "with great power, comes great responsibility". Mum doesn't want to say no to you and dad doesn't want to say no to mum, it's perfect!

Well after we have presented our wish-list to God we now call for some reinforcements, the saints. It's not that God can't say no to the saints. It's that He doesn't want to. In fact, He doesn't want to say no to us either. Thus the prayers on our wish-list, combined with those of the saints, stand a great chance of being answered as we requested. By venerating the saints, we are telling God, "remember these people, these saints of Yours? They also are praying for what we just asked for. And for their sake also, please forgive us our sins."

There is a beautiful tune used in this prayer. This beautiful tune draws out some phrases longer than others. It is interesting to note that the very first of these longer sections contains the words "Your Only Begotten", for we venerate the saints only in light of the image of Christ that is within them. The later sections repeat the exact same tune, though of course with different words, reminding us that the glory of the saints is nothing more than the reflection of the glory of the Only Begotten Son of God. The same way we ask friends to pray for us in hard times or during exams, we can also ask our heavenly friends who are members of the body of Christ to pray for me.

Recite the names

After the commemoration of the saints in the church, the deacon would exhort the congregation to, "recite the names of our holy fathers, the patriarchs who have fallen asleep..." At this stage a deacon would hold up a wooden board that had the names of all the patriarchs who had departed starting from St Mark the Apostle. These days, certain congregation members read it silently out of a book.

People, Places & Things

PRAYER FOR THE DEPARTED

From outside of the Orthodox faith looking in, it may seem bizarre that we are praying for the departed. Yet it is one of the oldest traditions of the Church. We hold in high regard those who have left this world to join the next and it is clear from biblical texts that God feels the same way. When God appeared to Moses in the burning bush, He introduced Himself as, "The God of Abraham, Isaac and Jacob" (Exodus 3:6). These patriarchs departed long before Moses yet God insisted that He was the God of the living and not the dead. How can this be? Well basically because Abraham, Isaac and Jacob are not dead at all but are alive with God. We say that they are in "the heavenly Jerusalem", "the Paradise of Joy", "the region of the living forever" as mentioned in the liturgical prayer. They are members of the Body of Christ and as members we should be praying for one another whether in this world or the next.

People, Places & Things

Peace be with you

Why does the congregation say to the priest "And with your spirit" after he says "Peace be with you all"?

Peace among the congregation means no fighting, hatred or judging of one another. Without this peace we cannot come forward to receive the Body and Blood of the King of Peace.

The priest prays "Peace be with you all" and he bestows peace by making the sign of the Cross. Through the supreme sacrifice of the Cross, Christ made peace between heaven and earth, and between man and his brother. As the people look to the

While mentioning the names of the departed and providing comfort to those who have lost someone, there is a deeper message behind this prayer. Yes, we pray that God may repose the departed souls into His fatherly embrace, but this prayer is also very much for us who are still alive. We say "And we too who are sojourners in this place (earth)..." and "As it was, so shall be from generation to generation..." We are prompted that this life will come to an end, and that all we see before us will cease to exist. It is a stark reminder to be alert, to "Watch therefore, for you know neither the day nor the hour in which" we may depart from this life (Matthew 25:13).

The priest puts a spoonful of incense into the censer when mentioning the name of someone who departed. This time the incense ascends to heaven, not only symbolising the ascension of our prayers but also the ascension of the departed soul into the loving embrace of the Father.

Cross, they bow. This reflects the fact that whatever takes away their peace is dissolved by the Cross.

Having received peace from God, the congregation also prays for the peace of God to fill the priest's spirit. The people cry out "and with your spirit". He too is a human being, subject to human emotions and weaknesses. He has to deal with difficult situations and people daily. He has the burden of the people thrown onto him and the responsibility of standing before God, accountable for his congregation. Thus, the wise priest clings to this response from the congregation! The prayers of all these people for him to find peace are much needed and appreciated.

THE RANKS OF DEACON

Originally a deacon was someone appointed by the Church to serve the people and aid the Apostles in whatever was needed, as seen in Acts 6. They were chosen based on some criteria as seen in 1 Timothy 3:8-13 "Likewise deacons must be reverent, not double-tongued, not given to much wine, not greedy for money, holding the mystery of the faith with a pure conscience. But let these also first be tested; then let them serve as deacons, being found blameless. Likewise, their wives must be reverent, not slanderers, temperate, faithful in all things. Let deacons be the husbands of one wife, ruling their children and their own houses well. For those who have served well as deacons obtain for themselves a good standing and great boldness in the faith which is in Christ Jesus." However, during the great expansion of the Church over time, there grew a need for the expansion and subdividing of the roles of the deacon. Although the term "deacon" should technically only be used for the actual rank that can administer the blood, the term deacon these days refers more to those people who wear white tunics during the liturgical services.

There are five ranks of deacon. Let's name them and review their modern day roles:

1)   Singer/chanter – This role is to learn and understand the hymns of the Church.

2)   Reader – To read the readings of the Church and explain them to those who need explanation.

3)   Subdeacon – The subdeacon is an assistant deacon. They should be responsible for things like the candles, censer preparation, books of the church, and priestly and deacon vestments. Should there for some

reason be a need to replace the church deacon, the subdeacon will often be selected. In the early church the subdeacon was responsible for the removal of "dogs and animals" from the church. With churches in country and farm areas this was probably a rather busy role. It is also the role of the subdeacon to stop heretics from entering the Church without the absolution of the priest or bishop, lest they corrupt the innocent minds of the people.

4)   Deacon – This is a consecrated role and is the first official rank of priesthood. The role of the deacon has changed dramatically over the years. Technically the deacon is the only one who should be chanting the non-priest responses in the altar. The deacon is also allowed to administer the blood and, in some parts of the Church, cense after the priest has placed incense into the censer. The deacon is also responsible for all the other ranks under him.

5)   Archdeacon – Technically there should only be one archdeacon in any diocese. Their role is the exact same as the deacon however they are responsible for all other deacons and are the head of all the deacons in a diocese.

The stole deacons wear on top of their tunics which in Greek is called a "patrachelion" (often pronounced "badrasheen" by our Arabic speaking congregation). "Patrachelion" means grace, which thus emphasises the grace bestowed on the deacons who carry this duty on their shoulders.

While our traditions are beautiful and meaningful, they must never become an end in themselves apart from a genuine inner life with Christ. A pure white tunia is of no value whatsoever if it hides an impure heart. And a neat patrachelion is no substitute for humble, self-sacrificial agape love.

THE RANKS OF PRIESTHOOD

"Hegumen"

In ancient Classical Greek, the word "oikon" (pronounced eh-kon) means "home", and "oikonomou" meant a homeowner. However, by the time of the New Testament, "oikonomou" had come to mean a steward, a servant or slave who was given the responsibility of managing the household finances and resources. This is also the origin of the modern English words "economy", "economist", etc. Over time, the original Greek pronunciation of the word evolved into "hegumen".

A hegumen is a senior clergyman who, in addition to his pastoral responsibilities as a presbyter (see below), is entrusted with the care of his church's finances and resources. In effect, he is to make sure that the flock has all the material resources needed to carry out its worship and service.

Thus, like the episkopos above, the origins of this title are quite humble! They reflect the nature of this office as one of humble service rather than power or authority.

"Presbyteros" or "Priest"

The word presbyter is another term used for priest. It literally means elder and can technically be given to all priests, hegumens and bishops as each of them are considered the elders of the church. The origins of this title can be traced back to Judaism and is seen even during the time of Christ as the chief priest, scribes and Pharisees were often referred to as elders. Today, as with the bishops, we pray that they complete their holy office in peace and love as well as in the wisdom and discernment of the Holy Spirit as St Paul instructed St Timothy, "Be diligent to present yourself approved to God, a worker who does not need to be ashamed, rightly dividing the word of truth" (2 Timothy 2:15). This is one of the greatest roles for all presbyters – priests, hegumens and bishops – to discern what is right and wrong. Thus, we pray that God guides these presbyters to "rightly divide the word of truth", a line that basically means, "may these men receive revelation from God to know what is correct and what is false teaching".

"DIAKONOS" OR "DEACON"

The title deacon stems from the word "diakonos" a title which predates the birth of Jesus and referred to one who executed the commands of another, especially of a master. In the time of the first church the deacons executed the commands of the apostles, now they do the works of the modern day apostles, the bishops.

All roles in the Church, bishop, priest and deacon, are roles of consecrated service and not honour. We do not place men to these roles to put them above others, but rather we ordain select men in order that they might be below others, below their congregation, so that they may serve them.

10. FRACTION AND CONFESSION

10. FRACTION AND CONFESSION

Before the priest prays the fraction there is an introduction that starts with, "Again let give thanks". It is an important prayer because it tells us what is it that we are doing throughout the liturgy. If you remember, the first part of the liturgy started with the thanksgiving prayer and now the last part starts with thanksgiving. Which points our attention to the fact that our job during the whole liturgy should be giving thanks and we should not stop doing so. In this prayer it says "Again", meaning we did it before and we will not stop doing it.

Even more interesting is the fact that the Greek word "Eucharist" itself means "giving thanks". So our main job in the liturgy is to give thanks non-stop to God.

THE FRACTION AND FINAL ADORATION

Most people don't get to see what is happening during the fraction so they think it is just another prayer, but the fraction, as the name may suggest, is the time in the liturgy when the priest breaks or fractures the body into pieces. The prayer that is said during the fraction changes depending on the season of the Church and the preference of the priest.

LIFE AND ANGUISH

God Himself does not change – He is the same yesterday, today and forever. But His effect on each person depends on the character of that person. His Body and Blood, while being life and light for those who love Him, is equally pain and anguish to those who desire to remain away from Him.

Fr Yacoub Magdy once shared this experience with me "Every new priest, the instant they touch the scars, the markings on the orban, for the first time, they are reduced to tears...I have never seen a new priest praying the first mass in his life and touching the scars of the Lord without being moved... Looking at these scars in eternity will be a tremendous source of joy."

So when we come forward for communion we must be holy. We are made holy through the gift of the Holy Spirit, working in our hearts and lives constantly – especially through the absolution of our sins in the sacrament of confession and the descent of the Holy Spirit in the invocation prayer. Only after this freely given and undeserved grace from God do we dare come forward to be united with His holy Body and precious Blood.

The way we apprach God on the altar should be fitting to the One who is on the altar. As St John Chrysostom says: "The wisemen, who were pagans and barbarians,

What the Fathers Say

"Now that the liturgy is accomplished, the Presbyter breaks the bread as our Lord first shared Himself in the flesh..."

– Fr. Tadros Yacoub Malaty

"For whomever
does not worship
the Body of
Christ, does not
receive It."

- St. Augustine

left their countries and homes and came to Jesus who was in the manger and worshipped Him in great fear. We, who are the sons of heaven, must at least imitate them. For they who saw Him in a manger inside a hut came in trembling and did not see anything of what you see now; you, who see Him not in a manger but upon the altar."

WHO BLESSES?

Why does the priest sometimes do the sign of the cross on the people and not at other times when he says "Peace be with you all"?

Around this part of the liturgy as we draw near to Holy Communion, whenever the priest says, "Peace be with you all", the priest turns away from the altar, facing the side, either the north or the south side, and bows. However, before the Institution Narrative, whenever the priest chants, "Peace be with you all", he turns to the congregation and does the sign of the cross. So why does the priest bless the people before the Institution Narrative but after this part of the liturgy he bows?

When a bishop visits a church, the bishop will be the one to lead the liturgy not the priests, as the bishop is more senior in rank than the priest. You may notice that even if a priest is praying that part of the liturgy, he will stop and allow the bishop to say the phrase, "Peace be with you all", while signing the congregation with the cross. It is not proper for a priest to bless the people in the presence of a bishop. Likewise, how can a priest or a bishop bless the people when Christ Himself is now physically present in the church in the form of bread and wine? So after the Institution Narrative, the priest moves out of the way when he says, "Peace be with you all", because we say that Christ Himself is blessing us at this moment. He is putting His hand over us. Christ is saying "Peace be with you all". Just as He said this to His apostles after His resurrection (John 20:19), likewise He is saying to us in this moment.

THE CONFESSION

Words spoken with conviction have such a power to motivate and change people. Jesus turned Levi the tax collector, a traitor to the Jewish people, into St Matthew the Evangelist and the author of the first gospel account, with the loving yet simple words of conviction, "Follow Me" (Mark 2:14). When something deeply and profoundly true is spoken with belief and conviction, then those words can break a stubborn mind and melt a hard heart.

This is that part of the liturgy. The moment of belief and conviction where it all comes together. The confession.

What the Fathers Say

The entire sanctuary and space around the Altar are filled with the heavenly powers who come to honour Him Who is present at the Altar

— St. John Chrysostom

What the Fathers Say

Be sure to keep the purity and peace of your heart, to be able to behold the Lord your God.

– St. Ephram the Syrian

TILL THE LAST BREATH

"Amen. Amen. Amen. I believe, I believe, I believe, and confess to the last breath". The first line by the priest is the most convicting line in the liturgy. What does he confess to the last breath? What do we believe in? The priest speaks with belief and conviction that what is present in front of us is the Body and Blood, "the life-giving Flesh of... Jesus Christ." The congregation confess in their hearts the same words, affirming their faith in what the priest is praying.

"To the last breath"! We do not say this lightly. For thousands of years, many believers literally kept the faith till their last breath. The martyrdom of Coptic Christians is said to have been very extreme. Faithful followers of Christ chose to give up their lives on earth rather than deny their faith. It is said that the blood of Coptic Christians flowed through the streets of Egypt. It is only because of their confession till the last breath that we have the Church before us today. But what about us?

Most of us aren't confronted with life or death situations for our faith. Many of us say that we would die for our faith; however, more difficult than this is living for our faith. Martyrdom may take a moment, but will we die daily for Christ? Will we, till the last breath of each day, confess with conviction that we believe? We need these words to resonate not just in front of the altar, but in our lives. In the face of temptation, we will not partake of evil because, "Amen. We Believe." In pain, we refuse to lose hope because, "Amen. We believe." When we fall we rise up because, "Amen. We believe." In times of despair and rejection, we will not stumble because, "Amen. We believe." We will not just die for God, we will live for Him! We will not just proclaim with our mouths but confess with our hearts, "Amen. Amen. Amen. I believe. I believe. I believe... till the last breath".

What do we believe?

THE REAL DEAL

What is present on the altar IS THE REAL Body and Blood of Emmanuel our Lord, not a mere symbol or a representation only, but the actual body and blood! The bread and wine in front of us is the real deal! The legitimate body and blood of Jesus Christ our God. How incredible! How great is God's love for us! It wasn't enough for Him to come from heaven to earth. It wasn't enough for Him to be born in a manger and live a life of poverty. It wasn't enough for Him to be insulted and murdered by His creation. It wasn't enough for Him to descend to Hades and raise the souls of the righteous. But in His incredible love He comes down to us individually, despite our separation from Him, and in the form of bread and wine He descends into our inner depths that we may be one with Him. He doesn't want even a tiny gap of separation between us but total

> **What the Fathers Say**
>
> Since Christ Himself has declared the bread to be His Body, who can have any further doubt? Since He Himself has said quite categorically, This is My Blood, who would dare to question it, and say that it is not His Blood? Therefore, it is with complete assurance that we receive the bread and wine as the Body and Blood of Christ.
>
> – St. Cyril of Jerusalem

The Eucharist is the Flesh and Blood of Our Saviour, the Flesh which suffered for our sins and which the Father raised from the dead.

– St. Ignatius of Antioch

union and intimacy. He wills to totally abide in us that we may totally abide in Him, to the point of being one with us through the consumption of His real Body and real Blood in the form of bread and wine. For this we are overwhelmed with joy and thanksgiving.

ASCENSION OF THE KING

As the priest proclaims the confession, he is holding up the Body of Christ for all to see and worship. We are seeing our King and God, and bow down in reverence and worship. We are at peace, knowing that this King and God will protect us and provide all we need to be satisfied, like food, shelter, but more importantly to be holy as he is holy.

This lifting of the Body of Christ is reminiscent of the ascension of Christ forty days after His resurrection. It is as though the disciples looked up and then bowed down in wonder on the Mount of Olives as they witnessed the ascension – as Christ's body is slowly rose up into the clouds and was hidden from their view. As he performs these actions, the priest continues the confession prayer. This is also a section that relives the important moments in the life of Christ. One can imagine the memories rushing through the minds of the disciples as their Lord was lifted away from them during His ascension. These same thoughts should be going through our minds. Jesus is our life, and we literally see His life flash before our eyes while the priest recites: "this is the life-giving Body that Your Only-

Begotten Son, our Lord, God and Saviour Jesus Christ took from our lady, the lady of us all, the holy Theotokos Saint Mary. He made It One with His Divinity without mingling, without confusion and without alteration. He witnessed the good confession before Pontius Pilate. He gave it up for us upon the holy wood of the cross, of His own will, for us all..."

11. Communion and dismissal

APPROACHING THE HOLY BODY AND BLOOD

The Body and Blood, of course, is to be approached in reverence. There are certain practices we can do to help revere the mysteries. There is a nice prayer before partaking of Holy Communion that should be prayed and can be found in the agbia (book of hours). Probably the best time to pray this is while lining up to partake of the mysteries.

The entire benefit of the liturgical service can be lost in a couple of minutes of irreverence while lining up. If you have finished the prayer, then a good practice is to say the Jesus prayer (My Lord Jesus Christ the Son of God have mercy upon me the sinner) or various other short prayers. When it is your turn to partake, you should bow down before the body and blood in worship.

Most people are unaware of this but as the priest or deacon is administering the holy mysteries they are saying "the Body and Blood of Emmanuel our God" to which we should reply out loud or in our hearts "I believe" which is another confirmation of our belief that this is the body and blood of Christ.

THE HOLIES FOR THE HOLY

As the priest begins distributing the mysteries, he turns around and raises the paten twice towards the congregation saying "The Holies for the holy", while the people respond, "Blessed is He who comes in the Name of the Lord".

This is an announcement to all that this is indeed the holy body and blood of Christ. We are reminded in previous prayers that those who wish to partake of the holy body and blood must themselves be holy. As the priest holds the body up high, our eyes are drawn above in longing and desiring to be made worthy to share in this heavenly feast. Of course we know that we can never make ourselves worthy of such a privilege, so our looking up is also a prayer, a request, a supplication to be counted as holy.

It is believed that St Macarius once was hit with the reality that he was not worthy to partake of holy communion. So he prayed and fasted much more rigorously than his already existing rigorous canon. After some days, an angel appeared to him and said, "Blessed Macarius, God is moved by your effort, but no matter what you do you will never be worthy of Holy Communion; even if you were perfect and never sinned. How could you be worthy of God? But it is purely out of God's incredibly loving grace that any human is allowed to partake of His body and blood." This message rings true amongst us today.

What the Fathers Say

When going to the Holy Mysteries, go with simplicity of heart, in full faith that you will receive the Lord within yourself, and with the proper reverence towards this. What your state of mind should be after this, leave it to the Lord Himself.

-St. Theophan the Recluse

We are not worthy of this great gift but God in His incredible love counts us holy enough to partake of Him. We receive Him so that He dwells in us. Thus, we taste the Kingdom of Heaven while we are here on earth.

THE DISMISSAL - RIVERS OF BLESSING

The priest then dismisses the angel of the oblation by throwing water over his head and reciting a short prayer. He then wipes his wet hand on his beard, asking God to bless his priesthood, and then the beards of all the other priests – sign of respect and blessing of the priesthood. He then goes around the church sprinkling water over the congregation.

Most people believe that this water is some kind of special blessing. Some even go to great and alarming lengths to be soaked with as much of that water as possible. Why? Have we forgotten that we have just partaken of the body and blood of Christ! Is there anything more blessed than that?

So why then does the priest spray the people with water if it's not for a blessing? This tradition is derived from Ezekiel 47:1-10,

"Then he brought me back to the door of the temple; and there was water, flowing from under the threshold of the temple toward the east, for the front of the temple faced east; the water was flowing from under the right side of the temple, south of the altar. He brought me out by way of the north gate,

---

What the Fathers Say

Many desire ahead of time to receive this or that from Holy Communion, and then, not seeing what they wanted, they are troubled, and even their faith in the power of the Mystery is shaken. The fault lies not with the Mystery, but with superficial assumptions.

–St. Theophan the Recluse

and led me around on the outside to the outer gateway that faces east; and there was water, running out on the right side. And when the man went out to the east with the line in his hand, he measured one thousand cubits, and he brought me through the waters; the water came up to my ankles. Again he measured one thousand and brought me through the waters; the water came up to my knees. Again he measured one thousand and brought me through; the water came up to my waist. Again he measured one thousand, and it was a river that I could not cross; for the water was too deep, water in which one must swim, a river that could not be crossed." – Ezekiel 47:1-6

From the above we see water flowing from the temple that begins from a depth as high as the feet of Ezekiel and rises all the way up till well above his head. The temple is the church and the altar therein. The flowing water is symbolic of the blessing received from the altar, namely the body and blood of Jesus; a blessing that develops throughout the liturgy and overflows in the congregation until it flows over them and drowns them with blessings through the partaking of the holy mysteries.

Thus the purpose of the water is not that it blesses us, for at this point we are overflowing with blessings, but rather it reminds us of the overflowing blessing within us. This is why the water should go on our heads or over us as it symbolises the very deep water of blessing we are now immersed in by the partaking of the Eucharist.

But wait! There's more!

"He said to me, "Son of man, have you seen this?" Then he brought me and returned me to the bank of the river. When I returned, there, along the bank of the river, were very many trees on one side and the other. Then he said to me: "This water flows toward the eastern region, goes down into the valley, and enters the sea. When it reaches the sea, its waters are healed. And it shall be that every living thing that moves, wherever the rivers go, will live. There will be a very great multitude of fish, because these waters go there; for they will be healed, and everything will live wherever the river goes. It shall be that fishermen will stand by it from En Gedi to En Eglaim; they will be places for spreading their nets. Their fish will be of the same kinds as the fish of the Great Sea, exceedingly many." – Ezekiel 47:6-10

The church is now seen as a river of blessings that is to flow into the sea of the world and heal the sea. The world is a very broken and damaged place and it needs healing! God has chosen you to perform His healing work. It is the responsibility of each member of the Church to go forth and spread the healing message of the gospel to all. We the Church are to go out into the whole world and share the blessing we have received from holy communion so that others may be healed.

Furthermore, we the Church are to be fishermen, ready and willing to catch all the fish (humans) of the world and bring them into the family of fish in the great river (the Church). Hence, the water sprayed on the congregation is not so much a blessing but rather a reminder of the greatest blessing of all, the partaking of the holy body and blood of Christ, and the spreading of this joy to the whole world. So the priest is not dismissing the congregation but in fact is sending them out to the world to bring healing to the rest of the world. It is an end of one liturgy and the start of another.

The congregation is then dismissed when the priest says, "The Love of God the Father, and the grace of His Only-Begotten Son Jesus Christ, and the gift and fellowship of the Holy Spirit be with you all. Go in peace the peace of Christ be with you all." At this point, the real work begins...

Father Elija also shared with me this story, "A lady from church was attending a mid week liturgy and not many people were present. She was closing her eyes in prayer. Then she opened her eyes and saw angels filling the church and standing around the altar. She was unable to stand out of awe and spent the remainder of the liturgy on her knees. I guess it means I should pay attention and get off my phone!" he continued during my fourty days at St Shenouda monastery

What the Fathers Say

Do not promise yourself anything. Leave everything to the Lord, asking a single mercy from Him — to strengthen you in every kind of good so that you will be acceptable to Him.

-St. Theophan the Recluse

The fruit of Communion most often has a taste of sweet peace in the heart; sometimes it brings enlightenment to thought and inspiration to one's devotion to the Lord; sometimes almost nothing is apparent, but afterward in one's affairs there is a noted a great strength and steadfastness in the diligence one has promised.

-St. Theophan the Recluse

Fr Wissa, taught us that even if the church is empty that we should go and spray holy water all the way to the back of the church and say "go in peace" even if we physically cannot see someone there - the angels and saints are in attendance."

THE END OF THE BEGINNING!

The service has now finished, but if you think that is the end then you kinda missed the whole point. The actual liturgy is only one aspect of the liturgical life and true Christian living. The end of the liturgy simply marks the beginning of the liturgical life. The world hungers and thirsts for the truth and we are all messengers of that truth. We need to take the messages of the liturgy, the messages of thanksgiving, reconciliation, grace, fellowship & unity, eternal life, and above all, the full love and communion between God and humanity. To partake of the body and blood of Christ and just live life like nothing had ever happened is really wrong. It is like treating Holy Communion like any other meal, like breakfast or lunch. The reality is we have now become united with Christ, and as Christ came into the world to save it, so we must also do the same.

As Christ spoke words of beauty on the mount, we too must speak godly words of comfort to all around us. As Christ served the children, sick, widows and all in need, we too must serve the children of God as faithfully as Christ. As Christ forgave, we must forgive.

As Christ rejoiced, we must rejoice. As Christ prayed, we must pray. As Christ loved, we must love. And as Christ died for the world, we too must sacrifice ourselves, in love, for the world around us, that as Christ raised us up, we may likewise raise others up to God.

As we sing in the liturgy, "Amen. Amen. Amen. Your Death, O Lord, we proclaim; your holy Resurrection and Ascension into the heavens, we confess. We praise You, we bless You, we thank You, O Lord, and we entreat You O our God." These messages we "Proclaim" and we "Confess", not just with our attendance, nor just with our words and actions, but with all that we are, we proclaim and confess the Truth of God throughout the whole world.

The day of communion with the Lord is a day of thanksgiving, joy and divine unity. It wouldn't really make sense to just go about business as usual then would it? We must take our participation in this gift very seriously, not out of fear, but out of love.

The spoon on our lips

In the Prophet Isaiah's vision (Isaiah Chapter 6), one of the seraphim took a live coal with tongs from the altar and touched the lips of Isaiah. The angel said to him, "Behold, this has touched your lips; your iniquity is taken away, and your sin purged". Similarly, when the spoon touches our lips as we partake of the Sacred Blood of Christ abouna says: "The Blood of Christ, given for the remission of sins, and eternal life to those who partake of them"

People, Places &Things

CLAP YOUR HANDS

You may notice that after the dismissal the priest does something a little odd. He walks around the altar touching the four corners clapping his hands. What is happening is the priest is praying psalm 47 which says, "Oh, clap your hands, all you peoples! Shout to God with the voice of triumph…" The priest is rejoicing in God and fulfilling this psalm by praising God and clapping his hands in prayer around the altar, thanking Him and giving Him glory for the great gift that was bestowed upon the whole Church.

I will end with what Fr Elijah Iskander has shared with me: "Thanksgiving and joy are two major themes of the liturgy from start to finish. One of my favourite prayers of the liturgy is when the priest at the end circles the altar and blows out the candles. He claps his hands as the psalm says "clap your hands all you people" filled with joy at the end of the liturgy. Also as the curtain is being closed, "keep the doors of the church open to the faithful". We are joyful before the liturgy, during the liturgy and after the liturgy in anticipation of the next liturgy."

CPSIA information can be obtained
at www.ICGtesting.com
Printed in the USA
JSHW082146171022
31772JS00001B/16